COUPLES THERAPY WORKBOOK FOR HEALING

COUPLES THERAPY
Workbook for Healing

Emotionally Focused Therapy Techniques to Restore Your Relationship

◆

Lori Cluff Schade, PhD, LMFT

callisto
publishing
an imprint of Sourcebooks

Interior and Cover Designer: Lindsey Dekker

Art Producer: Sara Feinstein

Editor: Brian Sweeting

Production Editor: Rachel Taenzler

Published by Callisto Publishing LLC C/O Sourcebooks LLC

P.O. Box 4410, Naperville, Illinois 60567-4410

(630) 961-3900

callistopublishing.com

Printed and bound in China

WKT 2

This workbook is dedicated to Steve Schade, my husband of 33 years, who has been a willing participant and good sport in my marriage enhancement adventures, and who regularly makes me laugh by randomly suggesting that we "talk about our feelings." I'm certain that he is the most noncritical and encouraging partner on the planet, which makes me feel incredibly lucky.

Contents

INTRODUCTION viii

HOW TO USE THIS WORKBOOK X

PART ONE: UNDERSTANDING RELATIONSHIP DISTRESS 1

Chapter One: **Attachment Theory Basics** 3

Chapter Two: **Negative Relationship Cycles** 25

PART TWO: NAVIGATING EMOTIONS 43

Chapter Three: **Regulating Emotions Together** 45

Chapter Four: **Core vs. Reactive Emotions** 55

Chapter Five: **Surging Sensitivity** 65

Chapter Six: **Emotional Bonding Conversations** 83

Chapter Seven: **Healing Attachment Injuries** 99

PART THREE: STRENGTHENING CONNECTIONS 115

Chapter Eight: **Maintaining Intimacy** 117

Chapter Nine: **Maintaining Bonds** 135

FINAL WORD 148

GLOSSARY 151

RESOURCES 154

REFERENCES 155

INDEX 162

Introduction

A few years ago, my husband and I were visiting potential rental properties with our realtor. As we were leaving the third apartment, my realtor remarked that he saw me studying the wedding photos in each residence. He was right. I'm magnetically drawn to wedding photos, because they usually exude joy and presumably represent a day of happy connection. I often wonder what people were thinking on that day, what surprises they have encountered since then, and what challenges they have overcome. I have been practicing as a marriage and family therapist along with raising my family for over 30 years, and have spent the last dozen years specializing in treating couples. The last few decades of groundbreaking research related to adult romantic attachment have informed a model I find effective for treating couples. This method is emotionally focused couples therapy, or EFT. It is considered a gold-standard treatment for partners in distress.

When I began seeing couples in therapy in 1989, I was frustrated with the interventions taught in my graduate program. The traditional behavioral techniques seemed to help with only mildly distressed couples, like newlyweds who had not yet entrenched themselves in negative patterns. However, I was soon faced with more challenging couples, most of whom had been married for a decade or longer and had histories laced with pain and insecurities. High emotion escalated rapidly with these couples and I soon found myself helplessly caught in a whirlwind of anger and hurt, feeling like I was more referee than therapist.

Even when couples reported improvement in sessions, it seemed inevitable that they would return the following week as distressed as ever, reporting that the communication skills we so carefully negotiated went out the window at the start of any argument. Nothing I did back then seemed to create durable change for couples. I developed a preference for individual therapy to couples' work because it was easier to manage the emotions in session.

About a decade later, my colleague told me about a new model that was developed by Dr. Susan Johnson. The model focused on the importance of the emotional bonds in our adult romantic relationships. I was immediately intrigued. I decided to get trained in the model, and finally felt empowered to treat couples. Where before I lacked confidence to choreograph events for positive change in session, I now had a therapeutic approach with clearly defined goals, stages, and interventions to help couples make long-term relationship changes. Sue Johnson's research and clinical work have been key components of a paradigm shift toward acknowledging the importance of romantic attachment bonds. Her work has also been key to integrating the exploration and acceptance of emotion into the therapeutic experience.

Today, EFT, backed by a large body of empirical research, has been applied to a wide variety of clinical presentations and populations. It has been used effectively with couples with depression, PTSD, childhood trauma, eating disorders, addictions, and chronic and terminal illness. It has helped couples struggling with aphasia, infertility, infidelity, sexual dysfunction, parenting challenges, and social and other anxieties. It has effectively aided remarried couples, culturally diverse couples, gay and lesbian couples, and couples with general relationship dissatisfaction. I have witnessed couples shift their negative patterns into more open, flexible, and secure bonding exchanges. EFT provides tools for couples to transform their relationships in remarkable ways.

There are already some very useful published resources to guide couples to understand and improve their relationships by undergoing EFT. This book is meant to be an additional resource to facilitate strong couple bonds. I see struggling couples make positive long-term changes every day, which drives my professional sense of purpose as I help couples restore loving bonds. I'm confident that through the explanations, examples, and shared experiences in this workbook, couples can access hope and see possibilities to shape resilient and fulfilling ties.

How to Use This Workbook

Emotionally focused couples therapy, or EFT, is a gold-standard treatment approach for couples, and it is supported by over three decades of research. It has been shown to alleviate couple distress and to promote positive emotional bonding experiences for healing. This workbook is designed as a theoretically sound guide for couples in general, to guide them through a specific process to increase relationship satisfaction.

EFT gives therapists and couples a structure of steps and stages for recognizing and disrupting negative patterns and for choreographing new bonding interactions. This workbook loosely follows those steps and stages. It can be used alone or as an additional resource for couples in counseling.

The book will explain attachment theory and its role in couple distress. You will then build on that information to understand how attachment distress leads to negative patterns of interaction, patterns that keep couples stuck in negative emotions. You'll be shown how to recognize those patterns. With increased awareness and communication in your own relationships, you will discover tools to stop the negative cycles.

After learning to slow down and step out of cycles, you'll learn more about emotional needs and how to reach out to each other to shape secure bonding moments. You'll gain skills for recognizing and dealing with deep injuries in romantic bonds. And you'll learn about the role of couple intimacy and sexuality in both negative and positive patterns.

Lastly, after successfully interrupting your negative cycles and creating positive interactions, you will gain ideas to keep your connection strong and healthy in the future.

WHO IS THIS WORKBOOK FOR?

This workbook is recommended for:

- Couples in long-term romantic relationships with a commitment to strengthening those connections.

- Persons of any ethnicity, age, gender, sexual orientation, religious belief, socioeconomic status, and education level, because EFT is based on universal human attachment needs.

- Couples working alone or as an enhancement to EFT couples therapy. Many couples in therapy benefit from additional readings and/or exercises to solidify the principles of their therapeutic process.

   This workbook is not recommended for:

- Couples who are currently pursuing a separation.

- Situations in which one or both partners is experiencing any type of intimate partner violence, including physical, sexual, verbal, or emotional abuse. These couples are advised to seek professional help.

- Couples in which one or both partners is actively engaged in an affair outside the relationship without the knowledge and/or consent of one partner. If the infidelity has stopped, couples can use this book to start the process of rebuilding their relationship, along with recommended professional help.

- Couples in which one or both individuals is engaged in an active addiction. An addiction can be a competing attachment in the relationship. The workbook will be most useful for couples who are actively working on sobriety from addictions, giving them a baseline of safety for them to attach.

- Anyone diagnosed with a severe mental health condition that is not managed. Individuals in these circumstances are encouraged to seek medical and/or mental health treatment.

- Being a replacement for EFT therapy. Attending sessions with a therapist can be highly beneficial for helping couples slow down and shift their positions.

EFT for LGBTQIA Couples

Attachment principles explain emotional processes between couples, gay or straight. However, individuals who identify as gay, lesbian, trans, or queer in a heterosexual world have often experienced a significant amount of trauma just from navigating a heteronormative society that is frequently hostile to them. They have often been shamed in the process of developing their sexual identities. Special care must be taken to explore any traumatic emotions accumulated over time. The intention here is to increase safety in owning and expressing vulnerabilities.

HOW DOES EMOTIONALLY FOCUSED THERAPY WORK?

- EFT is a direct result of Dr. Sue Johnson's groundbreaking and extensive research on couple distress. Her research specifically shows how couple distress develops and is maintained over time, and what specific processes allow couples to heal.

- EFT is cutting edge in its focus on understanding emotion as a driver of negative interactions.

- In EFT, couples learn how important their relationship is for providing comfort and emotional support. The context of a loving relationship allows partners to develop more secure attachment styles. Both partners learn to help each other regulate emotion and develop secure senses of self.

- Once couples understand their emotions in the context of negative patterns, they can begin to articulate their attachment longings. They can start to generate positive bonding moments that will serve to protect the relationship from future disruption.

- When partners are guided to slow down and understand their emotional reactions in the context of interpersonal interactions, they can access empathy and identify emotional needs. This naturally will increase clarity in their communication, without a handbook of specific communication rules.

- When couples feel threatened, they become more rigid and inflexible. As a result, they tend to protect themselves with narrow coping responses, keeping them stuck. EFT facilitates more flexibility and choice in behavioral interactions.

- The best teacher for all of us is experience. A couple's success in EFT is largely tied to developing enough trust to allow themselves to explore their feelings. With more trust, they are better able to take risks in having corrective emotional experiences.

- EFT facilitates change in attachment styles from insecure to secure, particularly through reducing avoidance. This is a huge research discovery, considering that attachment styles were historically believed to be fixed from childhood. Attachment styles can be changed.

A THREE-PART PROCESS

The format of this book generally follows the steps and stages of EFT therapy. The largest benefit will likely come if you proceed through the workbook in chronological order.

Part One: Understanding Relationship Distress

In the de-escalation stage, couples learn about attachment theory and how it explains distress in long-term adult romantic bonds. They will explore the components of self-perpetuating negative patterns and learn to deepen their understanding of their own emotions. Most important, they will identify coping behaviors, when they are triggered, and the impact those behaviors have on their partners. Once couples can deconstruct their negative cycles and routinely step out of those cycles, they can acquire skills to intentionally shape positive emotional bonding moments.

Part Two: Navigating Emotions

Couples will come to recognize the unique emotional sensitivities that trigger their negative patterns. They will learn how to identify and communicate their fears about which they feel most vulnerable and how to reach out to each other for specific types of reassurance and comfort. They will also discover ways to address deeper injuries in their past that keep them disconnected.

Part Three: Strengthening Connections

Issues around sexuality can become part of the bigger negative cycle. Ideas will be presented to manage and improve sexual connection. Finally, couples will identify their own lasting changes, their dream for the future together, and ways to maintain secure attachment and connection over time.

USING THIS WORKBOOK WITH YOUR PARTNER

EFT is not designed to focus on a partner's shortcomings. It is designed to help individuals uncover their attachment insecurities and learn to link them to emotional needs. It is designed to enable them to increase emotional risk-taking in the relationship. The idea is to help partners develop mutuality.

Be patient with yourselves and each other. I am often hesitant to send couples home with exercises if I think they might use them to hurt each other. If the exercises are causing conflict, it's okay to recognize that the emotions are high because this is a relationship that matters so much. You can revisit these issues and exercises later. Should you choose to seek out an EFT therapist, you can visit iceeft.com to find one near you.

One of the most important things to remember while working through this book is that the couple is meant to unify against the patterns that get them stuck. Everyone in close romantic relationships feels pain, and it's never a good idea to argue about whose pain matters more. The main thing is for couples to understand each other's pain. Then they can work together to build emotional safety for each other.

Create a couple's agreement that establishes the rules of engagement for approaching this work. Having a few simple guidelines for working together can be helpful.

- Some activities are designed to be completed individually ● and others are intended to be done together as a couple ●●. Some include both icons, meaning you can do them individually or together. Even with individual activities, you might decide it's worthwhile to share your individual responses to increase understanding.

- It may help to have a specific time during the week to work through the workbook.

- Recognize the power of slowing down. Learning new ways of interacting is just like learning any other new skill. It may feel awkward at first, but over time, slowing down enough to attune to your partner will provide new experiences and disrupt old habits.

- If one person wants to stop, honor that request and pick up again later at a mutually agreed-upon time. Have a plan for this beforehand, because when someone is emotionally flooded in the moment, it will be hard to choose a later time.

- Recognize the importance of having goodwill toward your partner. Cultivate curiosity, open-mindedness, and a readiness to feel, to express, listen, and interact.

PART ONE

Understanding Relationship Distress

Current research demonstrates that the quality of our bonded romantic relationships has a strong effect on our mental and physical health, for better or worse. Eli Finkel, author of *The All-or-Nothing Marriage: How the Best Marriages Work,* asserts that our society has shifted from a pragmatic view of marriage as an economic strategy for filling survival needs to a "love-based" view of marriage, with an emphasis on helping people meet their emotional intimacy needs. He describes a more recent cultural shift from 1965 onward to a "self-expressive" view of marriage in which marriage is expected to help individuals achieve personal growth.

Having higher expectations isn't a bad thing. As indicated in the title of his book, people with the best marriages are enjoying better marriages than ever. This is an exciting time to focus on romantic relationships. The explosion of research related to adult romantic attachment has and is helping us study the underlying mechanisms that both increase and soothe distress. When we understand how human beings develop and maintain intimate connections, we have more power to shape the quality of our relationships and, ultimately, our broader community connections. This chapter presents the foundational aspects of attachment and its role in romantic love.

• • •

CHAPTER ONE

Attachment Theory Basics

Our universal need for human connection transcends language, gender, sexual orientation, cultures, and ethnicities. Our drive to attach is human.

British psychiatrist John Bowlby is considered the father of **attachment theory**. He explained that we are born driven to develop emotional bonds with primary caregivers to ensure survival, and that we continue seeking those emotional attachments "from cradle to grave." He and researcher Mary Ainsworth spent years confirming the theory with experimental and observational research with babies. Now, an additional body of research from psychology, interpersonal neurobiology, affective neuroscience, and sociophysiology is providing us with an integrated view further supporting Bowlby's attachment theory.

Cindy Hazan and Phillip Shaver were the first researchers to study adult attachment and confirmed that we don't stop needing attachment in adulthood. We are driven to form deep affectional bonds with romantic partners to fulfill attachment needs. These bonds serve both as a safe haven from the world's stressors and as a secure base from which to explore the world with open curiosity. We monitor proximity to our **attachment figures**, and we experience anxiety when they are inaccessible to us. In short, our attachment figures give us confidence that we are not alone in a large, chaotic world.

WHY ARE SECURE BONDS NECESSARY?

Our primal drive to attach to people in relationships ensures our very survival, physically, mentally, and emotionally. Individuals with reliable attachment figures function better in all major measures of well-being. Reaching out for support and receiving a favorable response makes a complex, stressful world easier to navigate. In the words of scholar C. S. Lewis, "The typical expression of opening friendship would be something like, 'What? You Too? I thought I was the only one.'"

A few years ago, I was out in public with my husband in front of a large group of people and suddenly felt dizzy. Seconds later, I was lying on the floor gazing upward. I realized that I must have passed out, and I was flooded with embarrassment. I saw my husband standing beside me, talking to someone about calling medical personnel, which horrified me further. "Did I just pass out?" I asked, and my husband confirmed that I had and reassured me, but I still felt emotionally unbalanced. I reached up toward him for comfort and said, "Please hold my hand." He quickly sat next to me and took my hand in his, and I immediately felt better, physically and emotionally. This is an example of reaching out to one's partner for emotional reassurance and receiving a predictable positive attachment response. Suddenly, with my husband by my side, the world felt literally safer.

Some people are slow to acknowledge attachment needs, favoring independence. However, our interdependent relationships have a direct impact on our independence. It's common for me to hear clients protest that "I don't want to be needy." Paradoxically, however, research confirms that when people receive predictable positive attachment responses, they function more autonomously. When people have a safe base, the perceived safety allows them to take risks independently, away from the attachment figure. Sue Johnson asserts that this effective or constructive dependency is the "greatest strength" of humanity, and is the overarching goal of an EFT approach for any couple. Secure bonds are defined by couples executing this type of effective dependency in their relationships.

> *When people have a safe base, the perceived safety allows them to take risks independently, away from the attachment figure.*

This reminds me of many times back when I was in graduate school, from 1989 to 1992. I had a baby three weeks before starting a rigorous clinical and research-oriented program. My husband and I juggled our schedules to co-parent while I was trying to find time to attend classes, study, see clients, and manage the inevitable paperwork—and, oh yeah, be a first-time mom. Every time I went to my husband expressing my emotional distress, he responded, "Well, we'll get through it and I still love you." The words were simple but rich with meaning, and they gave me the encouragement I needed to hang in there. I knew he had my back and wanted me to succeed. I was not alone.

Recognizing Emotional Support

How do you and your partner emotionally support each other? Fill in the blanks and share answers with your partner.

1. When I have a bad day, my partner shows support by:

....

....

2. When my partner has a bad day, I show support by:

....

....

3. My partner provides encouragement by:

....

....

....

4. I provide encouragement to my partner by:

....

....

....

5. My partner provides emotional support by:

....

....

....

6. I provide emotional support to my partner by:

_____

_____

_____

_____

7. A time when my partner really had my back was:

_____

_____

_____

8. A time when I really had my partner's back was:

_____

_____

_____

9. My partner could better attune to my emotional needs by:

_____

_____

_____

10. I can better attune to my partner's emotional needs by:

_____

_____

_____

Strengthening Bonds

Explore opportunities for strengthening your bonds:

1. Do I see myself as someone who needs other people? Why or why not?

....

....

2. If I could reach out more readily with emotional needs, how might my relationship be impacted?

....

....

....

3. What is one way I can let my partner know if I have an emotional need?

....

....

4. Do I see myself as someone who easily attunes to the emotions of other people? Why or why not?

....

....

....

5. How do I feel about the idea that people can function more independently if they know a partner is accessible and responsive?

....

....

....

THE IMPACT OF EARLY ATTACHMENT EXPERIENCES

Our early attachment experiences are heavily influenced by caregiver responses because infants must adapt to caregivers to survive. Those experiences become part of our subconscious brain structures and they influence our beliefs and expectations about ourselves in relation to others. Every individual develops what Bowlby calls an **internal working model** to predict behavioral responses in interactions. The internal working model establishes one's positive feelings about oneself and one's ability to influence others in a relationship. Over time, we form attachment schemas about whether we are good and deserving of love, and of how trustworthy others are. Let's now focus on three **attachment styles** that are activated in relationships: Secure, avoidant, and anxious.

Secure

There is strong evidence of intergenerational transmission of attachment styles through experiences. Attachment depends on emotional communication. Infants develop **secure attachment** when they communicate needs and receive predictable, attuned responses. For example, an infant looks at her father, puts her hands in the air, and babbles, "Da, da, da," and the father makes eye contact, smiles at the baby, puts his hands up, and repeats back a variation of "Da, da, da." These responses decrease discomfort and increase positive emotions, thus aiding emotional regulation. Infants learn that relationships are a source of support, and that they can influence their caregivers. The result is a visceral sense of calm and competence. Attuned caregiver responses will help children restore emotional balance quickly. Those children, when grown, will likely have learned to become attuned caregivers for their own children.

Avoidant

In contrast, caregivers who are unresponsive or misattuned are likely to shape insecure styles. Infants will then minimize or amplify attachment need. Parents who inhibit, ignore, or rebuff their children's calls for emotional connection are likely to teach their children an **avoidant attachment** style. These parents are often uncomfortable with physical contact. In those cases, infants and children minimize their own attachment needs and seem to turn inward and self-soothe. Instead of communicating, they inhibit their emotional needs. As children, they tend to avoid closeness in interpersonal relationships. They are likely to become adults who persist in deactivating attachment needs and maintaining distance from others.

Anxious

Anxious parents are also misattuned. They aren't as openly rejecting as dismissive parents, but they are unpredictable and insensitive to children's emotional needs. Infants in these situations will amplify their **anxious attachment** needs with hypervigilance. The anxious protest might be visible in tantrums. These babies can be difficult to soothe. They seem to form the expectation that comfort won't be reliably available, so they maintain chronic emotional protests to elicit potential caregiving. They also seem slow to explore their surroundings, as if uncertain that caregiving will be available upon return. Infants who exhibit this style tend to become adults who monitor their romantic attachment relationships with the same type of chronic hypervigilance, and they seem to protest disconnection by displaying intense behaviors quickly and aggressively.

While attachment styles can be persistent, they aren't permanent. Recent research demonstrates that we are always being shaped. Corrective attachment experiences in the present can reshape older attachment styles. Couple relationships are an ideal laboratory for understanding and shaping more secure attachment relationships and behaviors.

Think about your life. Who were the people who cared about your well-being and responded to your needs?

When People Were There for Me

Although we start in infancy with one or two main primary caregivers (usually our parents), by middle childhood, we can get attachment needs met by other people. Some children who perceive that no one was there for them may identify a Higher Power as an attachment figure. Can you identify times when various people were there for you?

	When did this person offer you encouragement?	When did this person provide comfort?	Identify a time when this person was warm and nurturing.	When did this person sense that you needed emotional support?	When did this person normalize your emotional experience?
Mother					
Father					
Grandmother					
Grandfather					
Sibling					
Friend					
Teacher					
A Higher Power					
Other					

ANGIE AND RAJESH EXAMINE ATTACHMENT HISTORY

Before I questioned Angie and Rajesh about attachment experiences, I had the sense that they both had learned to be fiercely independent. Both were productive, competent professionals. However, they struggled when it came to identifying emotional needs. They took pride in independence and both agreed that needing people was "weak."

Neither had any recollection of turning to anyone for comfort or reassurance in childhood. Angie said, "I always took care of myself. I don't know why. That's just how it was." Her parents went through a high-conflict divorce when she was seven years old, and she didn't want to add any more stress to the family situation in the ensuing chaos. "I held things in," she explained, "I could see my mom was so stressed out with all the younger kids, so I didn't want to add to her burden." She became like another parent, anticipating her siblings' needs to manage the stress. She felt safe with her grandparents, but they lived in another state. She began hanging out at a friend's house as much as possible "because things were peaceful over there."

Rajesh grew up with his sister and a single mother in India and remembered that they were often worried about having enough food to eat. He would try to help by selling odds and ends, but said that he, like Angie, couldn't share his fear with his mother because he knew she was already worried. "What good would it have done?" he asked. "She was doing the best she could, and since my good-for-nothing father abandoned us, I was worried she would disappear, too. I didn't want to be needy then, and I still don't. You have to count on yourself."

When I explained the dependence paradox, that people function more autonomously when they know they have someone to count on, they both understood why that made sense, but having needs still felt risky. Neither had a precedent for reaching out emotionally. It was new in therapy for them to explore their relationship vulnerabilities and to learn to ask for help while under stress. They were comfortable managing their emotions alone.

Childhood Attachment Experiences

Recalling your childhood attachment experiences, reflect on the extent that you answer yes to each question:

1. As a child, I felt like I had someone I could go to when I needed comfort or encouragement.

2. I felt like I could count on someone to be there for me most of the time.

3. Even though my parents had stress, I still felt like I could go to them with my troubles.

4. I can think of at least one person I could go to for emotional support.

5. I learned that it's okay for me to reach out and let someone know if I need emotional support.

6. My experiences led me to believe that in general people can be trusted.

7. I grew up believing that I deserved to have my emotional needs met.

8. I had someone looking out for my best interests.

9. If I went to someone for emotional support, I was sure to get a positive response.

A Deeper Exploration of Attachment

Write down a time when you really needed someone for emotional support, comfort, or encouragement, and didn't necessarily have anyone there.

....

....

....

Who do you wish had been able to be there for you?

....

....

....

If you were guiding this person in the best way to comfort or reassure you, what would you say to them?

....

....

....

Knowing what you know now, write down what you would say to your child self to provide comfort or support in this situation:

....

....

....

ATTACHMENT IN ADULTS

In adult attachment research, attachment is generally examined in two dimensions: attachment-related anxiety and attachment-related avoidance. People high on the anxiety end tend to worry excessively about the availability of their partners, while those high in avoidance tend to prefer keeping people at a distance. Secure adults generally exhibit low anxiety and avoidance, while being high in anxiety or avoidance is associated with a type of insecure attachment. Some people exhibit **disorganized attachment**, which is a pattern of expressing high anxiety but then turning away or failing to trust reassurance when it is offered. Let's now explore the three basic categories of secure, anxious, and avoidant attachment.

Characteristics of Securely Attached Adults

Securely attached adults tend to have the highest-quality relationships, characterized by longevity, trust, commitment, and interdependence. They freely communicate their emotional needs and are available to meet their partner's needs. They believe that they are worthy and lovable, and are confident that they have an impact on their interpersonal relationships. They see others as basically trustworthy. They can approach their own feelings and their partner's feelings with curiosity, while regulating their own emotions. They tolerate closeness in relationships but also feel comfortable functioning autonomously. They are flexible and can shift between pursuing independent goals. They can also work interdependently in social groups as well as in close relationships.

Characteristics of Anxious Attachment

Anxiously attached partners constantly monitor their importance in the relationship. They are sensitive to emotional cues and quickly jump to conclusions about other people. They often become panicky when they are not near their partners. They can be repetitive and intense in their needs for reassurance about being loved and tend to imagine catastrophic scenarios in their relationships. Because their reactivity to those imagined catastrophes feeds their proximity-seeking behaviors, they are often viewed as "needy." Their hypervigilance can feel controlling to their partners. When worried about abandonment, they can become demanding and threatening, sometimes engaging in hostile and aggressive acts to get a partner's attention. They constantly worry that they will be rejected and/or replaced.

Identifying Anxious Attachment

How often do you exhibit an anxious attachment style in your relationship? Circle answers using the following scale:

1 = Never
2 = Occasionally
3 = Sometimes
4 = Often
5 = Almost Always

1. When I'm not around my partner, I'm worried that they could be interested in someone else:

   1   2   3   4   5

2. It's common for me to worry that I don't matter in this relationship:

   1   2   3   4   5

3. I spend a lot of time worrying that my partner will leave me:

   1   2   3   4   5

4. I worry about being abandoned:

   1   2   3   4   5

5. I find myself monitoring my partner's movements to make sure I still matter:

   1   2   3   4   5

6. I'm afraid that I'm difficult to love:

   1   2   3   4   5

Characteristics of Avoidant Attachment

Adults who display a high degree of avoidance tend to suppress attachment needs. They have learned to distract themselves and will create distance to manage their attachment discomfort. They pride themselves on self-reliance and don't tend to reach out to other people for help. They often feel uncomfortable when relationships get too close and may end relationships that require what feels like too much commitment. They also tend to rebuff the emotional needs of their partners and avoid or withdraw when pressed for deep emotional conversations. Maintaining deep, long-term relationships may be especially difficult for those entrenched in this attachment style.

Identifying Avoidant Attachment

How often do you exhibit an avoidant attachment style in your relationship? Circle answers using the following scale:

1 = Never
2 = Occasionally
3 = Sometimes
4 = Often
5 = Almost Always

1. When people start getting too close to me, I become uncomfortable:

   1   2   3   4   5

2. My partner always seems to want to spend more time together than I do:

   1   2   3   4   5

3. I prefer to rely on myself rather than depend on others:

   1   2   3   4   5

4. I feel uncomfortable when my partner wants to have conversations about our emotional connection:

   1   2   3   4   5

5. My partner tells me that I seem emotionally distant:

   1   2   3   4   5

6. If my partner complains that we are too distant, I have ways of distracting myself:

   1   2   3   4   5

Recognizing Behaviors and Attachment Style

Place an X in the square representing the attachment style illustrated in each of these scenarios:

	Secure	Anxious	Avoidant
Kai was feeling worried about his job security amid an economic downturn, and he described his fears to his partner, asking for reassurance.			
When Lily was missing her recently deceased mother, she expressed her grief to her partner, and he validated her loss and moved in to comfort her with a hug.			
Jin put a tracker on her partner's car because she was sure she was visiting an old girlfriend despite her reassurance otherwise.			
Tonya's boyfriend told her he wanted to have a talk about the future of their relationship and whether they were both committed, and she verbally dismissed his request and delayed coming home to avoid the conversation.			

Answers: secure, secure, anxious, avoidant.

HOW INSECURE ATTACHMENT STYLES CAN INTENSIFY CONFLICT

Sometimes attachment styles can become part of negative cycles in relationships, a topic addressed in the next chapter. It's not uncommon to see people with different attachment styles in a couple relationship, and they can end up polarizing each other as part of a pattern. This pattern is visible in the following story:

Allison and Jim came to therapy three years into their relationship when they were concerned about an escalating pattern of conflict. Despite her ease with expressing her emotions, Allison described some difficult attachment experiences growing up. She reported feeling "abandoned," and exhibited some ongoing anxiety about Jim leaving her. Jim seemed to have a more avoidant style, consistent with his report that as a child he would "go numb" when his parents would scream at each other. He learned from this that he had to take care of himself because no one ever seemed to notice that he had emotional needs.

Their last argument was typical of their different attachment styles. Jim left to get gas at a nearby gas station five minutes away. When he wasn't home an hour later, Allison called his cell phone, which went right to voice mail. Then, she started frantically texting him with no response. By the time he got home, Allison was in a frenzy.

He said, "She started screaming at me the minute I walked in, accusing me of hiding another girlfriend from her. It was crazy." He said he had seen an old college buddy at the gas station that he was talking to, and his phone had died, so he didn't know she was trying to reach him. "Yeah," she said, "but you know I have abandonment fears, and you didn't even try to comfort me or make me feel better." She explained to me, "He knew I was upset, and he could have comforted me, but instead, he just looked at me and said, 'I can't talk to you if you're going to be like this,' and he left again—almost like he just wanted to punish me. He really did abandon me." Jim cut in, "Stop being so dramatic. I didn't 'abandon' you. I just left until we could calm down." He did admit that since then, he has been avoiding talking about their relationship because "that always ends in disaster."

Allison's fears of abandonment drove her hypervigilance about her value to Jim, which came across as "needy." The more panicky she got, the more he felt "smothered" and wanted to escape or avoid emotional discussions, which drove up her fears. This maintained a negative cycle.

A.R.E.

Dr. Sue Johnson introduced the acronym **A.R.E.** to help couples think about their emotional responsiveness. John Bowlby described "accessibility" and "responsiveness" as behaviors that reinforce security in attachment relationships. To those two concepts, Dr. Johnson added "engagement," which describes the two-way involvement in emotional bonding sequences, increasing attachment security. Her book *Hold Me Tight* explains this acronym in more detail.

A few of my peers and former mentors, Dr. Jonathan Sandberg and Dr. Dean Busby, along with Dr. Keitaro Yoshida, worked with Dr. Johnson to create an instrument to measure these sets of behaviors. While not an official EFT assessment, ongoing research confirms that it is associated with higher relationship quality.

The acronym A.R.E. stands for:

Accessibility: How available are partners to each other?

Responsiveness: How well do partners respond to emotional needs?

Engagement: Do partners stay involved and close?

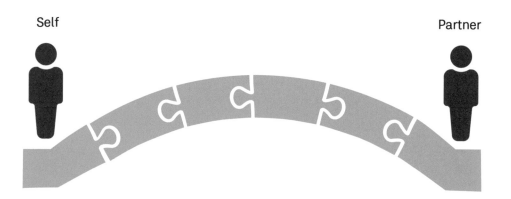

Self   Partner

A.R.E. Assessment

Think about the following questions as they relate to A.R.E.

Self:

1. I try to be available to my partner. (Yes/No)

2. It's not hard for my partner to get my attention. (Yes/No)

3. I try to listen to understand my partner's emotional needs. (Yes/No)

4. I'm glad when my partner reaches out, so I can show I care. (Yes/No)

5. When I'm uncertain about what my partner wants, I can be curious and ask questions to gain clarity. (Yes/No)

6. I feel empathy when my partner is distressed. (Yes/No)

Partner:

7. My partner tries to be available to me. (Yes/No)

8. I'm confident that if I really need my partner, I can get his/her attention. (Yes/No)

9. My partner really listens to me when I reach out emotionally. (Yes/No)

10. My partner seems glad to know he/she can help me. (Yes/No)

11. My partner is curious and asks questions to gain clarity when I am struggling to express myself. (Yes/No)

12. My partner empathizes with me when I'm distressed. (Yes/No)

Discussion Questions

Answer these questions about how you can improve attachment behaviors in your relationship:

1. How can I make myself more available to my partner?

   ....

   ....

2. How can I check in with my partner to signal that this relationship matters?

   ....

   ....

3. Are there ways I can be clearer about my emotional needs?

   ....

   ....

4. How can I let my partner know that I am reaching out because I value them?

   ....

   ....

5. What questions can I ask when I am confused or overwhelmed by my partner's emotional needs?

   ....

   ....

6. How can I increase my empathy for my partner?

   ....

   ....

TYING IT TOGETHER

Now that you have a basic understanding of attachment theory, you are ready to learn how attachment distress drives negative patterns in relationships. The next chapter will explain the nature and process of those negative patterns in relationships, how to step out of them, and how to keep them from taking over.

Key points:

- Human beings are born helpless and develop attachment bonds with caregivers.

- High caregiver attunement and responsiveness form the foundation for secure attachment.

- Attachment styles learned in infancy tend to persist throughout childhood, but reparative attachment experiences can reshape attachment expectations and behaviors.

- Adults use their romantic emotionally bonded relationships as a secure base in much the same way that children use an adult caregiver as a secure base, to provide refuge and to promote autonomous, exploratory behavior.

- Securely attached individuals display flexibility and competence in maintaining interpersonal relationships as well as in functioning autonomously.

- Anxiously attached individuals tend to closely and chronically monitor relationships and may be aggressive and difficult to soothe when they fear abandonment.

- Avoidantly attached individuals tend to favor independence and feel uncomfortable needing people and being needed.

- Adult attachment can be conceptualized in the acronym A.R.E. for accessibility, responsiveness, and engagement.

- Partners who can predict that their needs will be met will function more autonomously.

• • •

CHAPTER TWO

Negative Relationship Cycles

We don't end up in close romantic relationships by mistake. Most of us naturally seek closeness with partners who are accepting and supportive. Throughout relationship development, we share at deeper levels as we disclose parts of ourselves and are accepted. The mutual exchange creates safety and trust. Couples feel most secure when they have confidence that they can reach out for and receive emotional support. In the early stages of relationship development, people tend to be attentive to each other and find ways to cooperate and accommodate one other, fostering initial trust and safety.

Unfortunately, the world is filled with constant demands for attention. As couples attempt to balance their various competing work, family, and social demands, they inevitably miss emotional cues. This emotional misattunement is more often a result of distraction than intentional disregard. Regardless of intent, a lack of responsiveness can be perceived as a rejection. As people experience both small and large rejections from each other, the hurt from those rejections negatively impacts their willingness to take emotional risks. That's when partners begin protecting themselves from pain, and reciprocal problematic relationship patterns emerge. We are so finely attuned to our partners that we can create negative cycles before they even start, just by acting "as if." As partners protect themselves, they generally communicate less vulnerably and clearly, and sometimes these self-protective measures create a sense of distance that can be threatening to the relationship.

RELATIONSHIP CYCLES

Like flipping a switch, the first sign of distress can launch a couple into a predictable **negative cycle.** Both partners react to the disconnection by using coping mechanisms that in turn exacerbate the pattern, creating a negative feedback loop. They react to thoughts and feelings with behaviors that create reactivity in their partners. The reactivity becomes reciprocal. Over time, the repeated mutual experiences construct cycles that are faster, more intense, and anticipatory. They seem to take over and keep couples stuck in painful impasses. That's why it's so important to help couples unify against the commonly repeated cycle as the enemy, rather than against each other.

Sue Johnson identifies three major types of negative cycles associated with couple relationships, which she calls "Demon Dialogues," in her book *Hold Me Tight*: "Find the Bad Guy," "Protest Polka," and "Freeze and Flee."

Dr. Scott Woolley came up with the infinity loop for illustrating how couples continually react to each other and use coping behaviors to maintain negative patterns:

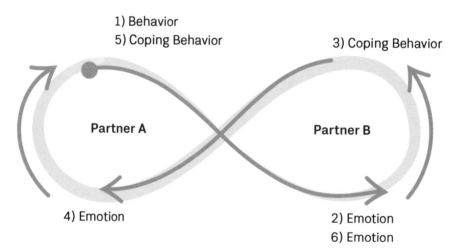

1) Behavior
5) Coping Behavior

3) Coping Behavior

Partner A

Partner B

4) Emotion

2) Emotion
6) Emotion

In this example, I refer to potential steps that might trigger a negative relationship cycle:

1. Behavior: Partner A uses a tone of voice

2. Emotion: Partner B feels hurt and irritated

3. Coping behavior: Partner B calls Partner A a name and leaves the room

4. Emotion: Partner A feels frustrated

5. Coping behavior: Partner A raises their voice and follows Partner B into the other room

6. Emotion: Partner B's emotions are overwhelmed and they feel powerless and hopeless. They now cope by refusing to answer until Partner A gives up and goes away, leaving both partners with mutual emotional distance, pain, and isolation.

The Pursue-Withdraw Cycle

The most common pattern with which therapists are faced is the **pursue-withdraw cycle**, also referred to as a demand-withdraw or criticize-defend. In terms of Demon Dialogues, it is called the "Protest Polka," so named because both partners are protesting a loss of safe connection in the relationship. Pursuing partners are often sensitive to emotional distance in the relationship, while withdrawers are routinely sensitive to emotional discord, both of which feel disconnecting.

When pursuing partners reach out to repair disconnection, a negative response from a partner fuels an intensified protest in the form of criticism, blame, demands, or threats. Their pain and fear in the disconnection appear as anger and aggressiveness to the withdrawing partner, who feels threatened by the increased conflict. The withdrawing partner will commonly stem the tide of emotions with defensiveness, stonewalling (refusing to respond), or pulling away. That retreat then fuels even more intensity in the pursuing partner, which is met with increased withdrawal, and around and around they go, paradoxically creating in each other the very responses they desire the least.

> *Pursuing partners are often sensitive to emotional distance in the relationship, while withdrawers are routinely sensitive to emotional discord, both of which can feel disconnecting.*

Over time, the couples become increasingly polarized and rigid in their responses. This decreases their potential for mutual flexibility, which would allow them to step out of the cycle and find solutions. The methods each partner uses to cope with relationship distress will trigger the very behaviors they are working so hard to avoid. Thus, the negative cycle seems to take over the relationship.

ENRIQUE AND PAULA IN A PURSUE-WITHDRAW CYCLE

The first time I met with Enrique and Paula, I had the sense that they perpetuate a pursue-withdraw cycle. "He's a robot," Paula passionately exclaimed, while her husband sat on the opposite side of the couch, arms folded, staring off into space. She continued, "We can never talk about anything important, because he doesn't want to deal with it. If I bring up any concerns I have in our relationship, he shows no emotion—he just gives me a blank stare like he's doing right now. Sometimes, he'll even get up and walk out of the room. I have no idea how to be in a marriage with someone who refuses to communicate. He doesn't care about me. I might as well be talking to the wall."

Paula's explanation was intense. While I suspected she was feeling lonely, hurt, and scared, I knew that her husband was reacting to her vivid display of anger. She clearly believed that she had no way to reach Enrique to be heard or validated. She seemed desperate. The more she talked, the lower he shrank in his seat. I could see him clenching his jaw, seemingly to manage his own emotions.

"What happens for you as your wife explains her perception right now?" I asked. "I hate it," he spat. "She says I don't communicate, but every time I try, she rejects my answers and gets angrier. I've learned that if I say nothing, she will eventually stop ranting and go away, but if I say the wrong thing, she'll rant even longer. I can never please her. I've tried everything to solve what she thinks are 'our problems,' but I'm starting to think she just needs a reason to be unhappy. She thrives on it—just like her mother."

"WHAT ARE YOU TALKING ABOUT?" Paula instantly escalated. "WHAT DOES YOUR BEING A ROBOT HAVE TO DO WITH MY MOTHER?" She turned to me, "See? He never takes responsibility for his own behavior. He refuses to deal with any-thing. I'm done." "Do you see?" he gestured as if on cue, "This is exactly why I can't talk to her."

Are We Stuck in a Pursue-Withdraw Cycle?

1. Does one of you typically bring up problems to discuss while the other one seems to want to avoid these potentially painful discussions? (Yes/No)

2. Does it seem like your discussion ends as soon as one of you shows strong emotion? (Yes/No)

3. Does it seem like you are never able to resolve the deep problems in your relationship because discussing them is too painful? (Yes/No)

4. Does it seem like as soon as one of you gives up, the other partner seems to finally move in closer to engage in a discussion? (Yes/No)

5. Does it seem like no matter what you do, your partner either becomes critical or shuts down and withdraws? (Yes/No)

If you answered "yes," to three or more of these questions, you are likely getting stuck in a pursue-withdraw cycle.

Protest-Protest Cycles

Cycles in which both partners escalate simultaneously, often fueling high-conflict interactions, are **protest-protest cycles** (or attack-attack). Dr. Johnson calls them "Find the Bad Guy." Each partner is desperate to be heard and explodes into a cataclysm of blame and counter-blame.

These cycles can be particularly alarming if there are children in the home who feel unsafe in the wake of aggressive emotional expression. In scenarios like these in my office, it's as if both partners feel cornered and will fight to the death. They seem to be hyper-focused on the other partner's flaws and stay stuck in their high reactivity.

SHALEENA AND JUSTIN IN A PROTEST-PROTEST CYCLE

When Shaleena and Justin came to therapy for the first time, they were arguing in the hall a short distance from my office. I sensed that they might be a couple that generated high volatility. They explained that they met in college and had instant chemistry. They remembered their initial courting stages as vibrant, adventuresome, and passionate. "You know that line about completing each other's sentences? That was us," Shaleena explained. Justin agreed, "Yeah, and we shared so many of the same interests. It seemed like we did everything together." After graduation, they married, and things were going smoothly until the birth of their first child. They explained, "It seems like after we had the baby, we just had so much more to argue about. We were both tired and new to this whole baby thing, and we were both overwhelmed."

While they could discuss their relationship calmly at times, at the juncture of any disagreement, the other partner jumped in boldly to correct the story. I felt stuck in a salvo of "That's not how it happened," and "Yes, yes it was!" Several times throughout early sessions of therapy, both partners disagreed vehemently and often. I could see both partners hurting, and yet I knew that they were reacting to the anger each was expressing. The spats quickly devolved into blame and name-calling. They attributed the worst motives to each other. "The bottom line," Shaleena explained, looking me in the eye, "is that he is just plain selfish. He was an only child, and his mama catered to his every whim and now he thinks that's what I should do, even if I have a baby to take care of. He doesn't care."

Justin blurted, "That's not true! I change all the diapers when I'm home and do more than most husbands I know." He glared, "She doesn't know how good she has it. And if I'm not helping, it's because nothing is up to her standards. I can't do anything right." "No, No, No, No, No," she began competing with him for airspace, and he mimicked back with "Yes, Yes, Yes, Yes, Yes," in an endless volley of finding who is to blame. I left early sessions feeling battle-scarred.

Exercise 2.2

Are We Stuck in a Protest-Protest Cycle?

Ask yourself these questions to determine if you and your partner create
this pattern:

1. If my partner raises their voice, is it important for me to get louder? (Yes/No)

2. Does it seem like we are both trying to prove who is right in our arguments? (Yes/No)

3. Do our arguments escalate quickly? (Yes/No)

4. Do we express enough anger that family members sometimes try to intervene? (Yes/No)

5. Does it seem as if we are both panicked that we will not be heard? (Yes/No)

6. Do we worry that we become out of control in these arguments? (Yes/No)

7. Does it seem inevitable when we are discussing something that it will turn into a large-scale fight? (Yes/No)

   If you answered "yes," to four or more of these questions, you are likely getting stuck in a protest-protest cycle.

Withdraw-Withdraw Cycles

This type of couple, what Dr. Johnson calls a "Freeze and Flee" couple, is easy to spot by their distance, which is often illustrated by sitting on opposite ends of the therapist's couch. In the **withdraw-withdraw** scenario, both partners seem to have given up. They use words like "tired" and "hopeless" to highlight the despair of feeling entirely unable to have any type of close, meaningful interaction. These couples present a particular challenge in therapy because they are so bereft of hope. Sometimes inspiring any kind of risk-taking or engagement can seem impossible. However, if these couples gain an understanding of their history and how their relationship evolved to its present state, they can generate the types of emotional bonding experiences that can remedy the distance.

CLARA AND JOCELYN IN A WITHDRAW-WITHDRAW CYCLE

Clara and Jocelyn explained that for eight years, they slowly drifted into a pattern of distance. Now they were questioning whether or not to stay together, but it seemed like neither had the energy to initiate a breakup. Both partners admitted that early in the relationship, Clara was the one to bring up problems to solve, but as soon as the emotions started to rise, Jocelyn, to avoid potential conflict, would end the discussion and disappear into another room. Over time, Clara gave up trying to discuss relationship problems. "What's the point? It doesn't matter what I do, she runs at the first sign of any emotion. It's like she wants me to have no emotion at all to have a discussion, and that's not going to happen, so I just don't even try to engage anymore. I really don't know if I have the energy to go on."

I expected Jocelyn to weigh in, but she sat, arms folded, staring at me. Eventually, when I asked if she saw things the same way or had a different perspective, she answered in a halting, mild voice. "I don't know," she mumbled, "I just can't think in these situations. Right now, I can't come up with the words to even explain what is going on inside of me."

"She never can," Clara piped in. "It's not just right now—it's all the time. I think it's an excuse so she can just do whatever feels comfortable, and if she feels comfortable, she thinks I should just be okay. Whatever. I don't even know why I'm here." The silent pauses between their sentences spoke volumes.

Are We a "Freeze and Flee" Couple?

1. It seems like we are just roommates living under the same roof, both lonely but hesitant to invite an interaction. (Yes/No)

2. It doesn't matter what I do or say, we will stay disconnected. (Yes/No)

3. I just don't care anymore. (Yes/No)

4. I don't have the energy for this relationship. (Yes/No)

5. My partner seems happier if we don't have contact, and I've decided to get my emotional needs met somewhere else. (Yes/No)

If you answered "Yes," to three or more responses, you are likely getting stuck in a withdraw-withdraw cycle.

Matching Couples to Patterns

Can you identify which couple fits in which pattern?

	Pursue-Withdraw	Protest-Protest	Withdraw-Withdraw
Katelyn is wondering if her husband remembers that it's their anniversary. Even though they have struggled lately, she wants to go out. She hints, "Do you remember what today is?" When Evan says, "No, should I?" Katelyn doesn't answer and walks in the other room. Evan shrugs his shoulders and leaves for work.			
Doug has told Collin over and over that he hates it when he invites people over without telling him. When Collin told him that he forgot a bunch of people were coming over in an hour, Doug exploded, blaming Collin for doing it on purpose. Collin screams back, f-bombs are flying, and they are both flinging examples of the other's character flaws.			
Mary is tired of feeling alone with household chores. She is afraid that she can't get everything done. Her anxiety is so high that when Antoine walks in the door, she fires off a list of things that need to be done. He rolls his eyes, walks into another room, and puts on his noise-canceling head-phones to make an "important call."			

Answers: withdraw-withdraw, protest-protest, pursue-withdraw

What Is Your Typical Cycle?

To understand what cycle you and your partner perpetuate, it is important to know:

1. How you react when your relationship is threatened . . .

....

2. And how your partner is impacted by your reactions.

....

A cycle is never one person's fault. It's an expression of ongoing **circular causality** in the relationship, which is always being shaped by both people. Fill in the following blanks to get a picture of what your relationship cycle looks like:

1. It seems like I can get thrown off-balance in this relationship when:

....

....

....

2. When my partner seems upset, I tend to cope with it by:

....

....

3. When I behave this way, it seems like my partner reacts to me by:

....

....

....

4. When my partner reacts to me this way, I feel:

....

....

5. The more I feel this way, the more I:

_____

_____

6. The more I do that, I'm guessing that my partner feels:

_____

_____

7. It seems like when my partner feels this way, the reaction is:

_____

_____

8. In short, the more I _____ , the more my partner

_____ , keeping us stuck with no solution.

HOW CYCLES BECOME SELF-PERPETUATING

While there are discrete categories for predominant types of cycles, some cycles are too complex to reduce to one category. Over time, some couples may even find that they switch positions in their cycles. Some couples switch positions according to certain subject areas, like sex, which will be discussed later in this book.

Identifying Your Cycle

Try identifying your cycle from a recent argument.

1. The thing that set me off was that my partner

    ....

2. I immediately felt

    ....

3. I coped with the situation by

    ....

4. My partner then may have felt

    ....

5. My partner coped with their difficult feelings by

    ....

6. Which resulted in my feeling

    ....

7. So as the cycle continued, the more I .... , the more my

    partner ....

Identifying Complex Responses

In the following scenarios, see if you can identify the trigger, the resulting emotion, the partner's coping response, the resulting emotion, and the counterresponse.

1. Miles (Partner 1) realized that his wife, Shandra (Partner 2), wasn't coming home when she said she was, so he fed the kids the dinner he made and angrily threw away the leftovers, thinking that if his wife was too inconsiderate to let him know she would be home later, she could get her own dinner. When she walked in the door, he immediately yelled, "Thanks for letting me know you would be home late!"

   Before she could explain, he continued, "I cannot believe how selfish you are. If I had known I would be married to a narcissist, I would have called off the wedding." She attacked back with, "Are you serious right now? You're not even going to ask why I'm late? You call me selfish and narcissistic? What kind of husband is so arrogant that he thinks he doesn't even have to find out what happened before he unleashes on his wife? Right! A narcissistic one. Takes one to know one!"

   Partner 1 (Miles) Trigger: *Shandra coming home late without telling him.*

   Partner 1 (Miles) Emotion: *Hurt, dismissed, alone, angry.*

   Part 1 (Miles) Coping Response: *Throwing away Shandra's dinner and yelling at her when she walked in.*

   Partner 2 (Shandra) Emotion: *Hurt, alone, misunderstood, angry.*

   Partner 2 (Shandra) Coping Response: *Yelling in counterattack, name-calling.*

   Cycle Type: *Protest-Protest*

2. Bill forgot the milk on the way home from the grocery store. When he walked in the door and saw his wife in the kitchen, he remembered. He approached his wife, "Shoot, honey—I know you told me to get the milk, and there was an accident, and I had to take a detour and didn't pass the grocery store, and totally forgot." Debbie, who needed the milk for a dessert she was making for the kids' bake sale the next day, exploded with, "I should have known I couldn't count on you. Why did I think that for once you would actually come through for me?" Bill walked out of the room and avoided her for the rest of the night.

Partner 1 Action That Triggered Partner 2: ....

....

Partner 2 Emotion: ....

....

Partner 2 Coping Response: ....

....

Partner 1 Emotion: ....

....

Partner 1 Coping Response: ....

Cycle Type: ....

TYING IT TOGETHER

By identifying the cycle you and your partner perpetuate, you have increased your understanding and ability to fight the cycle together, instead of allowing it to take over. Later chapters will address how to step out of negative cycles more specifically.

Emotion is the fuel that drives negative cycles between couples. Because our romantic bonded relationships matter so much to us, anything that threatens that security seems to sound an alarm bell, triggering the self-maintaining patterns of reactive behaviors, emotions, and more reactive behaviors. Much of this happens outside of our awareness. It's much easier to observe what a partner is doing than to observe ourselves when stuck in negative cycles.

Understanding attachment, negative cycles, and our emotional tendencies gives couples the ability to slow down, understand, and fine-tune their emotional responses. They can better increase flexibility to more efficiently co-regulate their emotions. Part 2, which follows, will delve deeper into emotions and their role in romantic bonded relationships.

Key points:

- When individuals reach out to their partners and don't receive attuned responses, they experience raw emotions that drive reactive coping behaviors.

- These coping sequences are repeated often enough to become predictable negative patterns.

- Partners coping with reactive emotion end up counter-triggering their partners in an endless feedback loop of self-maintaining emotional triggers and coping behaviors. These feedback loops keep partners stuck in their positions, without resolution.

- The most common cycle is a pursue-withdraw cycle in which partners take on polarizing positions over time. One partner is usually bidding for more closeness while the other is trying to prevent destructive conflict. The other two major types are "attack-attack" and "withdraw-withdraw."

PART TWO

Navigating Emotions

While there are varying theories and categories of emotion, we'll start with the basics. Dr. Paul Ekman identified six core emotions associated with predictable facial expressions evident across cultures. They are happiness, sadness, fear, disgust, anger, and surprise. Other theories include additional emotions, like shame, which are not necessarily associated with specific and universal facial expressions. Emotion is also shaped by language and is continually being constructed by individuals managing their experiences. Charles Darwin explained that expressing and recognizing emotions is biologically adaptive in social contexts. In short, it is a matter of survival.

Emotions are also a driving force in forming romantic bonded relationships. "Feel-good" emotions may compel us to form loving bonds in the first place, but the advantages of pair-bonded relationships transcend that benefit. Adult attachment relationships also offer enormous potential to co-regulate distressing emotions through those bonds. The next chapter explains how understanding emotions can help couples structure their relationships and improve their overall functioning.

. . . .

CHAPTER THREE

Regulating Emotions Together

Humans are fundamentally emotional beings. Every day, we have multiple opportunities to feel emotions. The way we respond to them highly influences our success in social situations. Moderating emotional responses instead of reacting thoughtlessly helps us stay connected to the world around us and allows us to safely and competently deal with daily stressors.

Emotional intelligence is the ability to have awareness about emotions and respond in a way that lets us keep our balance with those around us. Much of this emotional regulation happens individually as we increase awareness of our own emotions, attune to others' emotions, and remain flexible enough to stay engaged. However, recent research has shown that we can learn to **co-regulate**, or improve our emotional regulation through access to social relationships. In a romantic partnership, this means becoming attuned to each other's emotions and being able to provide and receive emotional support. When couples understand the benefits of co-regulation, they can work together to overcome stress more efficiently than they could alone.

FEELING ALL THE FEELINGS

A quick perusal of any bookstore self-help section will confirm our culture's seeming obsession with happiness. It's common for segments of our western culture to grant privilege to positive emotions with platitudes like "Choose Happy." In fact, some might say we have a culture preoccupied with positivity, sometimes at the risk of minimizing or denying the full range of human emotions. I have heard well-meaning self-help experts even suggest that to stay "happy," it's advisable to "avoid people expressing negative emotion."

I find this nothing short of alarming. One of our greatest strengths as humans is our ability to identify distressing emotions in others and generate empathy to offer support, encouragement, and soothing. Avoiding negative emotions prevents us from experiencing profound human connection.

Before I give the impression that I'm hating on happiness, I want to clarify that, yes, there are benefits to positivity. Positive emotions are an important stress buffer for mental and physical health and promote general well-being. Accessing positive emotions soothes autonomic arousal, or the nervous system's response to anxiety. This increases our ability to regulate our emotions and be responsive to our partner's emotional needs. One marker of resilience is the ability to use positive affect through humor, hope, optimism, gratitude, and creativity.

When we grant privilege to happiness, however, we fail to recognize that all emotions are giving us information about our needs. It's common to see attempts by individuals and even social science communities to disregard or minimize emotions. However, emotions are an integral part of our behavioral and cognitive processes. Rather than avoiding, suppressing, or being overwhelmed by emotional states perceived as negative, we must seek to understand them. That way, we can use our emotions to better understand our needs, which in turn helps us strengthen our bonded relationships.

THE POWER OF CO-REGULATION

In love relationships, most of us recognize the drive to develop and maintain connection with people who make us feel positive emotions. I once attended a training for depression in which the presenter began with the tongue-in-cheek assertion that the best way to alleviate depression was to "get someone to fall in love." We generally associate the term "falling in love" with a cocktail of positive feelings. Inevitably, however, distressing emotions will arise, and one of the advantages of pair-bonded relationships is the opportunity to co-regulate distressing emotions, attuning to our partners, and coordinating our movements to soothe the distress and restore well-being.

The power of co-regulation in a safe couple relationship was confirmed by neuroscientist Dr. James Coan of the University of Virginia. He executed a hand-holding experiment in which he monitored activity in the brains of female subjects using functional magnetic resonance imaging (fMRI). Subjects were told to expect a low-level shock, and brain activity was evaluated in three conditions: while they were alone, holding the hands of strangers, or holding the hands of their significant others. The hypothalamus, which is the part of the brain that regulates stress hormones, was significantly less active when the women were holding the hands of their partners in happy relationships. In essence, this demonstrates protective health factors for people in high-quality relationships.

Regulating emotions with a partner in a trusting, safe relationship is much more efficient than trying to do it alone.

In an exciting more recent study, Dr. Sue Johnson teamed up with Dr. Coan and others to study the impact of EFT on couples' neural processes in a similar experiment. Women in distressed relationships had fMRI scans in the same conditions as the previous experiment. When they expected the painful shocks, holding their partners' hands didn't seem to alleviate the stress of getting shocked. After completing a course of EFT couples therapy, learning to understand their negative cycles and emotions so that they could disrupt their negative patterns and create safe bonding experiences, the women were again evaluated under the same conditions. After working with EFT therapists, the women's brains showed lower stress activity. Regulating emotions with a partner in a trusting, safe relationship is much more efficient than trying to do it alone. Couples really can reshape their relationships to offer safety in distress.

Sharing Events Associated with Positive Emotions

Write down a few instances when you experienced positive emotions around shared events.

....

....

....

1. Share one (or more) of these experiences with your partner.

2. Listen to your partner's experiences.

3. What was it like to hear your partner share recollections of positive memories?

....

....

....

4. Another marker of resilience is the ability to find positive meaning in a negative event. Think of when you found positive meaning over time in an event that initially elicited negative emotions.

....

....

....

5. Take turns sharing your answers to this question with your partner.

6. What was it like to hear your partner describe their answer?

....

....

....

Emotions and Action Tendencies

Emotions are generally associated with particular action tendencies. Although responses can be regulated and changed, there are typical behaviors associated with certain emotions. For example, anger is associated with an aggressive response, while fear is associated with avoidant responses. Positive emotions, like joy, are associated with approach/exploratory responses. One way to regulate emotion is to increase awareness of one's own action tendencies.

Identify a time when you have felt each of the following emotions. Write down the event and mark where in your body you felt this emotion. What were you saying to yourself while feeling this emotion? What did feeling this emotion make you want to do? This is an action tendency. Fill out the following exercise to increase your awareness of your emotional responses:

Emotion: Anger

Situation: _____

Where I felt it in my body: _____

What I said to myself: _____

What I wanted to do: _____

Emotion: Sadness

Situation: _____

Where I felt it in my body: _____

What I said to myself: _____

What I wanted to do: _____

Emotion: Fear

Situation: _____

Where I felt it in my body: _____

What I said to myself: _____

What I wanted to do: _____

Acceptable Emotions

People learn a lot in their family environment about which emotions are acceptable and what the rules are for having and expressing those emotions. Families transmit these rules both explicitly and implicitly by showing approval or disapproval of certain emotions, and by modeling expression of emotions.

A few years ago, I was visiting with a family in Chile in their home, and the husband, Diego, learned that I was a therapist. He told me a story that is an excellent example of how families send messages about emotions. He explained that when he was a young teenager, he learned about depression at school, and went home and told his mom that he had learned what was wrong with him—he had depression. His mother invited him out to the back porch, where he said she proceeded to slap him on the head and sternly said, "Depression is for rich people. Get to work." She handed him a broom to start sweeping the porch. He laughed while he told the story, and I could see the humor, but I could also see how that message was likely to be transmitted to future generations, minimizing very real feelings.

Consider the following list of emotions and circle those emotions that were acceptable to express at home.

Anger	Disappointment	Insecurity	Sadness
Anxiety	Discouragement	Jealousy	Shame
Boredom	Fear	Nervousness	Weakness
Confidence	Frustration	Pride	Worry
Confusion	Hurt	Rejection	

Shaped by Emotion

Reflect on the following questions to increase awareness about how you have been shaped to think about emotion:

1. How was positive emotion expressed in my family?

2. What did my family teach me about emotions in general?

3. How did my family express anger?

4. What messages did I get about anger?

5. How did my family express sadness?

6. What messages did I get about sadness?

7. How did my family express hurt feelings?

8. What messages did I get about hurt feelings?

9. What are some of my beliefs about negative and positive emotion now?

TYING IT TOGETHER

Gaining awareness of your emotions and the role they play in close relationships will help you become more flexible in how you express yourself and respond to your partner. Learning to co-regulate emotion with a trusted partner has a profound overall impact on individual and relational health. Now you're prepared to dig a little deeper to see how emotions drive the negative patterns that can take over in a relationship, and to recognize ways to manage emotions and step out of negative cycles.

Key points:

- Emotions are at the core of love relationships.

- One of the advantages of **pair-bonded relationships** is that you can co-regulate emotions.

- Learning to co-regulate emotions in a good relationship is more efficient than trying to regulate emotions alone.

- Emotions drive related action tendencies.

- Increasing understanding of our own emotions increases self-regulation.

- Understanding what we learned about emotions in our families of origin can increase our awareness of our own emotional responses.

• • •

CHAPTER FOUR

Core vs. Reactive Emotions

To understand emotional responses, EFT helps couples see the difference between core and reactive emotions. **Core emotions** are initial, direct responses to situations. **Reactive emotions** are reactions to these core emotions. These are expressed through coping responses that are easy to see. For example, anger is easy to spot, but is frequently a coping emotion in response to more vulnerable feelings like hurt, fear, or a sense of powerlessness.

THE ROLE CORE VS. REACTIVE EMOTIONS PLAY IN NEGATIVE CYCLES

Emotion is fast—faster than our ability to make sense out of events with language. Our finely attuned systems viscerally pick up cues about our partners' emotional states from facial expressions, vocal tones, and outward behaviors. Much of the time we react to what we see without even realizing it.

ANNA AND TED AND ACKNOWLEDGING NEGATIVE FEELINGS

Anna and Ted explained this exchange to me in a joint therapy session. Anna's husband was a building contractor, so his small-business profits occasionally varied according to the movements in the broader economy. In a significant economic downturn, he lost several contracts and was struggling to find work. At the end of a long day, his wife was looking at their budget and expressed worry about having enough to make their house payment. He flared, "I'm sick of hearing what a failure I am!" When his wife described the incident to me in a session with her husband, I asked the husband if besides anger, he might also have been feeling worry, or anxiety or anything related to that. "Yes," he agreed. "She has no idea how much stress I'm under all the time. I feel ashamed, and I doubt my ability to take care of my family. I'm not sure what to do. It's terrifying, actually." Anna had no idea he was trying to manage all these feelings, because he had never talked about it. He had learned there was no value in acknowledging negative feelings because all that did was "make you feel crappy," and yet, because he was having the feelings, they surfaced as volatile anger.

Recognizing core emotions is important because they are connected to the actual emotional attachment needs of the individual. We will review emotional needs more thoroughly in a later chapter, but for now, consider the story of Anna and Ted. Ted was experiencing self-doubt, shame, powerlessness, fear, and hopelessness about his ability to make a living. As we unpacked his emotions, he realized that he was needing to know that Anna could still love him and help support him even if he wasn't making as much money as usual. He needed reassurance that he was more than a paycheck. When he could slow down for a minute and describe his experience, he had more awareness about what was going on and was able to help his wife understand. This is one way to interrupt a negative cycle. Anna could then get close enough to those softer emotions to offer support—the type of co-regulation discussed earlier. The reactive anger kept her at a distance, as reactive emotions often do. They protect people from further pain by keeping potentially threatening partners at a distance. They also prevent people from eliciting the soothing and support needed for regulation, and this keeps couples stuck in their negative patterns.

TANYA AND ANNA AND REACTIVE EMOTIONS

Reactive emotions are on the surface and are easily perceived by others. Unfortunately, these often become the triggers to which partners react, keeping the negative cycle going. Consider the following situation:

Tanya recently found out that her partner, Anna, had been sending text messages to a former lover complaining about Tanya and expressing her affection for the former partner. When Tanya was describing how she discovered the texts and how betrayed she felt, it was easy to see how angry she was. "I can't believe you would do this to me," she yelled at Anna, although Anna was sitting two feet away. Any observer might accurately label Tanya as furious. However, the rage was a protest of the hurt she felt from her partner's betrayal, and likely was also fear about the future of their relationship. In this case, the core emotions were hurt and fear while the reactive emotion was anger.

The couple explained that throughout the week when Tanya was reminded of the texts, she would find Anna and start yelling at her again. Anna reported, "She basically just wants to verbally beat me up, and I'm getting tired of it, so the last time she went after me, I got up and left."

Tanya agreed, "That's right. She confirmed that she will abandon me. I can't believe she did this to me after two years together."

The diagram on page 58 shows how Tanya coped with her hurt and fear by protesting it with anger. In her hurt and fear, she really needed comfort and reassurance, but instead of moving closer and comforting her, the anger triggered Anna into withdrawal. In the moment, all Anna could see was the wall of anger, and said it was like a "tidal wave and I will be destroyed if I stay." This unfortunately confirmed Tanya's worst fears of being unlovable, abandoned, and alone.

1. Behavior: Leaves

2. Emotion: Hurt, Fear

3. Coping behavior: Yelling, blaming

4. Emotion: Shame, regret, helplessness

5. Coping behavior: Leaves

6. Emotion: Anger

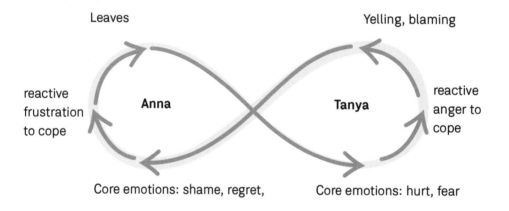

Leaves

Yelling, blaming

reactive frustration to cope

Anna

Tanya

reactive anger to cope

Core emotions: shame, regret,

Core emotions: hurt, fear

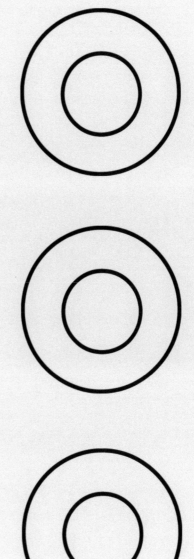

Identifying Core and Reactive Emotions

For each of the following situations, see if you can identify some core and reactive emotions. Write down the core emotions in the center and reactive emotions in the outer circle:

1. Sarah found out that her husband had been messaging his old girl-friend on Facebook. She confronted him by yelling at him and calling him a "selfish pig."

2. Karen had been sharing finances with her partner Shanelle. She found out Shanelle had a secret bank account that she had been hiding and was unwilling to dis-close what she was using it for. Karen screamed at her before packing a suitcase to go sleep somewhere else.

3. Joe asked his wife to pick him up from work at 5:30 p.m. so he could go pick up his car from the mechanic before they closed at 6:00. When she showed up at 5:50 p.m., he launched into a verbal tirade about how he could never count on her to do what she said she would do.

Reflecting on Anger

1. When is the last time you remember expressing anger? ....

....

....

2. As you think about it now, was there another softer emotion underneath
   that may have been related to the anger?

....

3. Can you think of a time when you tried to suppress having an emotion
   because it was so uncomfortable?

....

....

4. As you think about it now, what was the soft emotion that felt necessary
   to suppress?

....

5. What might make it easier to share core emotions with your partner?

....

....

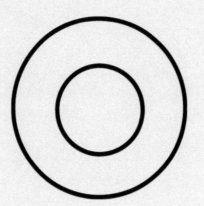

JAVIER AND BELLA

Javier and Bella had been coming to therapy for four months. Javier had been married once before, and Bella had been married twice before to men who were physically and verbally abusive. Javier reported that it seemed like any time he had "any emotion," Bella would shut down and run away from him, and he was starting to feel like he had to "be perfect" for her to stay in the same room.

While Bella admitted that she was sensitive to displays of anger, because she immediately felt like she was back in her abusive marriages, she described struggling to engage with Javier when he was angry because "everything in me sees him as potentially dangerous. I can't move toward him when he's like that." He immediately snapped at her with, "Stop punishing me for your exes' mistakes, and if you wanted to be married to a robot, you should have married a robot!" While she physically stayed in the room, her emotional retreat was palpable.

He was loud. So loud, in fact, that my own visceral sense as a therapist was to retreat, but I recognized that his rage was masking hurt, sadness, fear, and probably shame. Instead of retreating, I slowly moved in closer. "I can see you are so upset," I said, "It makes so much sense to me that you are angry, and I am also seeing you in a lot of pain. You are also really, really hurting. Am I right?" I asked. He made eye contact with me and burst into tears while nodding his head. I lowered my voice. "I really want to know more about what is so painful under all that anger. Can you help me understand that?" His descriptions of the hurt, sadness, and worry that his wife would always see him as a "bad person," and always stay distant from him, seemed to draw her in.

When he was able to describe the longing he had for her to see him as different from her other husbands, and his desire to draw her closer for support, she was able to have empathy for his hurt and pain, and naturally felt compassion. When his emotional expression shifted from hard-edged anger to the real, softer emotions underneath, his wife moved closer and reached out and put her hand on his leg. She explained that she did see him as a good person, and said it helped her to be able to see this side of him instead of the anger that covered it up. The anger was nearly impossible for her to approach, but the hurt, pain, and shame were emotions she could move in closer to help him with. His anger, which helped him cope with the difficult softer feelings, was also preventing him from getting the comfort and reassurance he needed.

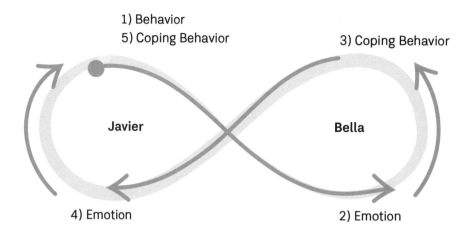

1) Behavior
5) Coping Behavior

3) Coping Behavior

Javier

Bella

4) Emotion

2) Emotion

1. Behavior: Javier (pursuer) is aggressive and attacks

2. Emotion: Bella (withdrawer)'s primary emotions are fear, hurt, and sadness. Her reactive emotions are feeling resentful and angry

3. Coping Behavior: Bella withdraws and shut downs, she is numb and distracted

4. Emotion: Javier's primary emotions are feeling ashamed, unloved, disconnected, unwanted, and lonely. His reactive emotions are frustration, anger, and resentment

5. Coping behavior: Javier responds verbal aggression and threats

TYING IT TOGETHER

We have discussed attachment, negative cycles, and the role that emotions play in driving couple interactions. The next chapter will give couples the opportunity to link emotions to personal and relationship history to understand why some situations flare up so quickly and what to do about it. We will explain how to use emotions to identify emotional need and we'll teach couples some strategies for reaching out to each other, reinforcing relationship safety.

Key points:

- One of the benefits of a romantic bonded partnership is to learn to co-regulate emotion with one's partner.

- Over time, people become finely attuned to emotional shifts in their partners.

- Partners have fast, recurring emotional triggers that drive coping behaviors.

- Frequently, the emotions that are expressed the most intensely are ways of coping with deeper hurts or fears.

- Core emotions, like sadness, hurt, shame, or fear, are the emotions that are often concealed behind reactive emotions like frustration and anger.

- Understanding the nuanced differences between emotions can increase both emotional self-regulation and co-regulation potential.

CHAPTER FIVE

· · ·

Surging Sensitivity

Have you ever had a moment when suddenly you felt a surge of emotion, even though the content of your argument seemed trivial? Or perhaps there was a moment when the expressed emotion seemed surprisingly high? We all carry emotional sensitivities from our past and from our relationship histories; the past can become the present in an instant. Specifically, these sensitivities can usually be traced to moments when we felt rejected or left alone, deprived of comfort and attachment connection. In EFT, Sue Johnson calls these **raw spots**, and understanding them can help couples more readily regulate the intense emotions.

IDENTIFYING RAW SPOTS

I was on vacation with my husband last year, and on our way out the door of our hotel room, I dropped something. As I reached over to pick it up, my husband made a tsk sound—that sound when your tongue clicks against the roof of your mouth. I had an immediate visceral reaction. I doubt he even realized he did it. He wasn't upset at me, but interestingly, I felt bad inside when I heard that noise, like I had done something wrong. I realized that my father, who was overall a very warm parent, made that very sound to express his disappointment in something I did. Hearing my husband make the same sound generated the same terrible feeling I got when I was younger and hated disappointing my father.

When we came back to our hotel room, the memory of my husband making the sound flashed in my mind, simultaneous with the same visceral reaction as before. I knew this was not a big deal, but I decided to tell my husband, just to regulate my emotional reaction so I wouldn't continue to ruminate on it alone. I wasn't telling him to criticize him, but just as a matter of interest in something I noticed, to share my experience. He was as surprised as I was, since my father was rarely angry, and yet that sound metaphorically turned me into a sad five-year-old child in the present.

Why Does My Partner Choose to Live in the Past?

That's a nice idea, but we don't choose these emotions. Emotions are the result of a sophisticated body-to-brain, brain-to-body biofeedback system starting with an automatic visceral response. We can learn to regulate and manage emotions, but painful events from the past will come up in the present. Ignoring these reactions is a missed opportunity for emotional, mental, and relational growth and improved regulation of scary, disorienting emotions.

Why Should I Be Responsible for Attachment Failures That Occurred in Other Relationships?

You aren't responsible, but you do have a huge opportunity for shaping a new, safe attachment relationship by helping your partner understand their own reactivities and by meeting emotional needs in the present. I'm always trying to help partners see expression of emotion as an opportunity to create new positive bonding experiences. In a way, receiving emotional information from a partner is a bid for connection. If a partner is expressing emotion, something can be done about it. As a therapist, I am more worried when partners refrain from expressing emotions and try to hold everything in, or prefer to manage emotions alone, because it prevents the opportunity for emotional bonding. That's why it's so important to learn to express emotions in a way that draws partners in, eliciting authentic empathy.

Sensitivity Stories

I hear stories about similar sensitivities several times a month. Here are a few typical examples. Underline the raw spot for each one:

1. Anna and her husband Ahmed had only been married for a few months when she asked him to pick her up from a doctor's appointment. When he was 15 minutes late, he was shocked that Anna got in the car yelling about his unreliability. He couldn't believe she was this upset over 15 minutes. Later, Anna explained that her mother routinely forgot to pick her and her sister up from school, or would show up an hour late. She spent much of her childhood not knowing if her mother would show up or if she would have to find a way to call and remind her or go to a friend's house. She explained that when Ahmed was late, she started to have the same sick feeling in her gut she would get waiting for her mother.

2. Carlita reported that she felt highly anxious when she saw that Todd's sister had been texting him about a problem in her life. When she started questioning him about the texts, he got defensive and asked why she was interrogating him over a simple conversation with his sister. Carlita realized that the feeling she got was the same feeling when, earlier in their marriage, she found out that Todd was giving his sister money without telling her. At the time, she struggled with the deception and the fact that he was hiding things from her. Seeing their text exchange brought up the same feelings.

3. Joseph went with his partner, Mark, to a party. Halfway through, Joseph seemed to withdraw into sullen anger. On the way home, when Mark asked about it, Joseph accused him of caring more about being with other people than with him. Mark was shocked, because he had no idea what Joseph was talking about. Later, Joseph explained that a previous partner used to tell him how boring he was and ended up ghosting him in the relationship. He said that seeing Mark laugh with other people at the party brought up the same feelings of "my entire world collapsing," and he withdrew to try to manage the difficult feelings.

Reflect on Your Raw Spots

Think of a moment when you suddenly felt a surge of emotion or felt instantly thrown off in an unexpected situation.
Describe the situation:

....

....

....

....

As you think about it now, what emotion came up the strongest?

....

....

....

....

Did any other emotions come up?

....

....

....

....

Can you think of a time either more recently or in the past when you may have felt similar emotions? Describe the situation:

....

....

....

....

Share your answers with your partner.

Search for Potential Sensitivities

It's common for people to experience emotion in the present and not even realize that the emotion might be linked to previous times in their personal histories in which they may have felt similar emotions. For example, a husband who feels "bad" when his wife cries might realize that he had the same emotion when his mother was crying and he as a child felt overwhelmed and helpless to comfort her.

For each situation, can you guess at a potential past sensitivity that might be contributing to a current surging sensitivity?

1. Jacinda has a full-time job as an attorney while her husband has chosen to stay home with their three children. She walks in the door and sees that the children are eating in front of the television, even though she and her husband have agreed that they will limit television time and eat dinner together every night. She blows up.

Potential sensitivity from the past: ....

....

....

2. Katie's partner, Sheila, was frustrated with something she saw on television, and when she yelled at the TV, Katie said, "I hate it when you're like this," and got up and left to go into a different room.

Potential sensitivity from the past: ....

....

....

3. Kalani's wife forgot to bring his jacket to the outdoor concert, and he got immediately upset and yelled, "I can never count on you."

Potential sensitivity from the past: ....

....

....

BREAKING DOWN RAW SPOTS

In *Hold Me Tight,* Sue Johnson explains these sensitivities or raw spots by breaking down into steps the fast, immediate emotional reactions that we have. I have found that these steps help my couples gain awareness of each other's sensitivities by thinking about them this way:

1. We pick up on subtle cues that give us a sense of emotional safety or danger. Many of our most emotional experiences happen in an attachment context. That means successful connection is associated with soothing and feelings of safety, while failure to connect is associated with danger and painful emotions like fear, shame, and rejection. We are constantly scanning our environment to prepare for social interactions, and seemingly small cues can set off alarm bells if they have been paired with previous attachment failures. For example, Kim and Ethan are having a conversation when suddenly Kim looks at me and reports, "Well, see, now he's mad." I ask, "How do you know?" and Kim answers, "Because he does that thing with his eyebrows when he's mad." I didn't see it, but she was finely tuned to his facial expressions. The same is true of vocal tones. People react to a "tone of voice" quite often, regardless of the content.

2. Our bodies respond to the cues. As an undergraduate, I worked in a stress management biofeedback lab. I was fascinated with the sensitivity of some of the instruments for picking up indicators of stress in the body without my cognitive awareness. Emotions are associated with action tendencies, so they mobilize the body to prepare for those actions.

3. We make sense out of what our physiological experiences are telling us. For example, Marsha is stressed out after a long day, and she asks her husband, Maddox, to wipe off the kitchen table. He realizes that there have been many occasions when that "tone" has accompanied her telling him that he has disappointed her, which is painful for him.

4. We prepare for the action associated with the emotion. In response to what he thinks Marsha's tone indicates, Maddox's body reacts, and he escalates the situation by adopting an irritated tone to match hers.

Uncovering Sensitivities from the Past

Thinking about your past, what experiences did you have with these emotions at any of these time frames?:

	Rejection	Abandonment	Loneliness	Worthlessness	Betrayal
Grade School					
Junior High					
High School					
College					
Adulthood					

As you think about it now, do any of these sensitivities pop up in the present? Which ones?

....

....

Identify some cues that might throw you off balance, such as tone of voice or a look on a partner's face:

....

....

....

Write down some ways that your body responds in these situations:

....

....

....

What emotions come up in these situations?

....

....

....

What do you say to yourself in these situations?

....

....

....

Does it feel safe to think about sharing these sensitivities with your partner?

....

....

....

Importance of Parts

Sometimes, if we aren't ready to reveal vulnerable sensitivities all at once, it helps to think about our conflicting parts that want to do different things. For example, a part of you might want to share something to potentially improve the relationship, but another part might be hesitant because it feels too scary, and you might be worried that your partner could use it against you later.

If you find yourself hesitant to share your vulnerabilities, identify what the different parts of yourself are and what they want, and label them on the figure:

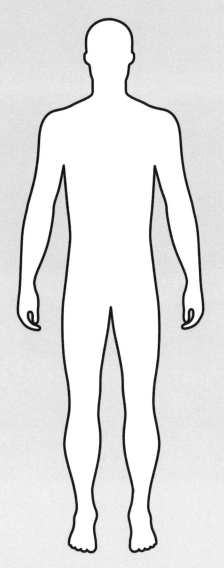

Part of me would like to be able to share these softer parts with my partner because it could benefit us by:

....

....

....

....

On the other hand, part of me is worried that if I share, then:

....

....

....

....

What would you need your partner to know to make it safe for you to share some of these sensitivities?

....

....

....

....

Can you identify a time when you were able to be vulnerable and find comfort with your partner?

....

....

....

....

Share this time with your partner.

DE-ESCALATING TO REPAIR DISCONNECTION

It's established in relational research that a couple's ability to repair the ruptures in their relationship is key to overall relationship quality. We all occasionally lose our emotional equilibrium, but partners can restore balance by working together to step out of their negative cycles and unify to work against those cycles when they seem to take over. I encourage couples to use these steps, outlined in *Hold Me Tight* by Sue Johnson, to fight their negative cycles together:

1. Stop the cycle by recognizing it and using language to invite your partner to try to step out of it.

2. Claim your own moves in the negative cycle. Let each partner notice what they are doing in reaction to each other.

3. Claim your own feelings in the negative cycle. Let each partner notice not just reactive feelings, but possible core feelings driving reactive behavior.

4. Own how you shape your partner's feelings. Let each person identify what it is they are doing to create reactive feelings in their partner.

5. Ask about your partner's deeper emotions. This one might be the hardest, because once stuck in a cycle, couples want to protect themselves. It helps to ask about your partner's feelings in a soft way, with authentic curiosity.

6. Share your own deeper, softer emotions.

7. Stand together as allies against the negative cycle.

My Own Cycle

The following dialogue is from a situation in my own marriage in which we were headed toward a typical negative pattern. I try to be congruent with what I ask clients to do, and so I used these steps to avoid further escalation of a typical pattern. I'm not setting myself up as the consummate expert, but hopefully it feels believable since it was real. I'm not going to lie, it wasn't easy. Both of us had to regulate emotion, but getting through the process helped set us up to step out of cycles in the future. I will identify the steps in our dialogue:

Me: Hey, before we go to sleep, can we talk about [insert potentially volatile topic, such as finances or children]?

Husband: Sure!

He gets in bed next to me.

Me: I was thinking [insert whatever fabulous idea I had for managing aforementioned unpleasant topic].

Him: I don't know, what about [insert opposing idea in a slightly raised tone, cuing me for a fight].

I match the raised tone and up the ante.

Me: Why do you always . . . ?

He adopts a defensive stance.

Him: Why do *you* always . . . ?

He gets up out of bed, standing now.

Me: WELL, *you* . . . [insert louder, angry response about his defensive stance]

Him: WELL, *you* . . .

He takes a few steps toward the door, places hand on doorknob.

Here's where I would continue the cycle by yelling back, and he would probably yell back before walking out the door, which would annoy me, so I might get up and follow him, or I might stew in my self-righteous anger before falling asleep.

Here's a diagram of how the cycle had started:

Behavior: critical tone

Coping behavior: Defensive withdrawal

Coping behavior: Get louder

Partner A

Partner B

Reactive emotions: Anger

Primary emotions: Panic, fear, hurt, rejection

Reactive Emotions: Anger

Primary emotions: hopeless failure

But since I was trying to be Super Congruent Authentic Marriage Therapist, I . . .

1. Identified that we were getting stuck in the cycle:

Me: Wait a minute. We are escalating into our pattern, and I'm really not trying to, but I can see that you are about to walk out the door.

Him: Yeah, because you're yelling.

2. Claimed my moves:

Me: I think I'm getting louder because I'm seeing you start to walk out, which brings on a panic response where I talk faster and louder, but I want to understand what you're feeling. [Pause to think.] Do I seem like I'm being critical to you?

Him: Pfft! Yeah! Totally critical!

Me: Wow. I'm surprised because I was really trying for the opposite. I guess I can seem critical to you really fast without realizing it. [I inwardly congratulate myself for regulating my emotions instead of yelling a reactive, "Critical?! If you want to see critical . . . !"]

3. Claimed my own feelings:

Me: I guess when I'm afraid you're going to just walk out, my fear turns into panic and you probably just see that I'm angry instead of that I'm really wanting to just try to discuss things with you without losing you and I'm afraid I can't.

4. Own how I shape my partner's feelings:

Me: When I'm getting panicky, you must hear a tone in my voice that you've heard when I've been critical, and you start feeling like I'm unhappy with you. Is that what you think is happening?

Him: Probably.

5. Ask about my partner's deeper emotions:

Me: I'm really sorry I'm having that impact on you. So, you worry that, whatever you say, it won't be the right thing, and you feel hopeless that we can solve anything?

Him: Yeah.

6. Share my own deeper emotions:

Me: I'm really, really not wanting to have that impact on you. My panic is coming from fear that I can't talk to you without pushing you away, so I am going to try to keep my fear from escalating so we can figure this out.

7. Stand as allies against the cycle:

Me: How about this? Since we are so sensitive to each other, how about if my fear starts to sound critical, you let me know so I know that you are being triggered. Can you try to let me know if my voice has that critical tone?

Him: [Thinking . . . Still Thinking . . .] Okay.

He walks back to bed, gets in, and we manage to have a conversation without getting into our typical pattern.

It might have been nice if my husband had been a little more engaged and disclosing, but the point is that by slowing down and deconstructing what was happening, we were able to keep our normal pattern from escalating and starting over again to have a more cooperative conversation. I'm certain that when he is emotionally activated, he loses words to describe what is happening. The process does get easier by slowing down and with practice.

Identify the Steps

Label each of the following pieces of dialogue according to which step
they represent.

1. I'm guessing you get more afraid than I can tell, right? Can you tell me more
about the abandonment feeling that comes up?

Step: ....

2. I'm wanting to move away because I'm getting that feeling that you will be
unhappy with me no matter what.

Step: ....

3. When it seems like you're unhappy with me, I feel totally inadequate.

Step: ....

4. Maybe if we slow down and watch our reactions, we can create safety together
to stay connected instead of letting our reactions get between us.

Step: ....

5. I'm guessing that when you see me start to move away, you probably get that
abandonment feeling, right?

Step: ....

6. Let's slow down a minute. We're getting into our cycle.

Step: ....

7. It's not just that I'm inadequate. I feel entirely worthless.

Step: ....

Changing ingrained negative patterns is not easy. At this point, the ability to
repair is more important than stepping out of a negative cycle every time. If you can
do it once, give yourself *lots* of credit and realize that it takes *a lot* of courage and
a lot of practice. Sometimes couples get overly discouraged when they have a success and suddenly slip back into old patterns. This will happen, and it is normal.
You always have more opportunities to shift negative patterns if you can be patient
with yourselves.

Answers: 1:5, 2:2, 3:3, 4:7, 5:4, 6:1, 7:6

Reflect on the Steps

Think of an incident in the last few weeks in which you and your partner got stuck in a disagreement (one that was relatively mild) and see if you can name the steps

for you and your partner:

Describe the incident:

....

....

What reactive feelings did you have?

....

What softer feelings did you have?

....

....

What reactive feelings did your partner have?

....

What softer feelings did your partner have?

....

....

What can you say to your partner to invite them into an alliance against the cycle?

....

....

TYING IT TOGETHER

Now that you understand sensitivities and have a template for slowing down arguments and unifying against negative cycles, you are ready to learn about building positive bonding events in your relationship to inoculate your partnership against stressors that might inflame insecurities.

Key points:

- Everybody has painful events from the past that can trigger emotional reactions in the present.

- Sharing these sensitivities can feel risky, but it can also help partners empathize and offer support.

- There are specific steps that couples can use to step out of their negative cycle, take ownership of the part they each play in the cycle, and unify together against the negative cycle.

- Be patient with yourselves. Changing cycles requires awareness, slowing down, and practice.

CHAPTER SIX

• • •

Emotional Bonding Conversations

This section focuses on intentionally building connection so you can reinforce emotional safety and security. This is important for shoring up the relationship and avoiding moments of great disconnect. The idea is that you are taking the time to figure out what your attachment longings are and becoming more comfortable with taking the risk of letting your partner know what those longings are so they can respond effectively. Dr. Sue Johnson refers to these conversations as positive emotional bonding conversations.

Some people think they are already reaching out for emotional needs to be met, but the reality is that they are often unclear. This increases the likelihood that the attachment cues will be missed. This makes sense. It is far less risky to communicate emotional needs obscurely. We feel more protected that way. However, when partners increase clarity so their partners can successfully read the cues and increase their responsiveness, they are engaged in an active, cooperative effort to build the relationship.

ARTICULATING EMOTIONS THAT MAKE YOU FEEL VULNERABLE

Elise was visibly upset in our session. She explained that earlier in the week, she had tried to send signals to her husband, Tyson, that she needed comfort, and he had ignored her. Upon further exploration, she explained that when Tyson walked into the room, she sighed heavily and "slammed cupboard doors," to get his attention. Elise thought "he should know" that by signaling distress in this way, she needed him to come close, ask what was wrong, and offer comfort. "He knows that I'm still sad about my sister dying unexpectedly a few months ago. Why couldn't he at least ask me what was wrong?"

Elise's actions were typical of how partners act when they feel too vulnerable to disclose deep emotions and needs. It felt less risky to stomp around, hoping that Tyson would notice. Then, at least if Tyson didn't pick up on her cues, there was the possibility that he didn't know, rather than that he didn't care and was purposely ignoring her. She agreed, "If I had told him up front that I was sad and needed comfort, and he walked out, it would have been way more rejecting." Unfortunately, those obscure signals that feel safer to send are usually too obscure to elicit the needed caregiving. None of us are mind readers. When I asked her husband about his experience, he said, "Yes, I saw her slamming cupboards, and I could tell she was upset, so I decided to leave her alone to calm down." He thought she needed space, which is what he said helps him when he's upset. His exit was not a signal that he didn't care, but that's what Elise interpreted.

One phrase that comes up repeatedly in couples therapy is, "If they loved me, they would . . ." I agree that it is an appealing idea to have partners completely attuned to our needs, but alas, it is entirely impossible. That's why, as an EFT therapist, I am trying to help couples articulate emotions that make them feel vulnerable and express related emotional needs. This increases the couple's possibilities for accurate attunement. Intentionally creating these moments can increase relationship security.

The positive bonding conversation facilitated in EFT has a few specific simple steps:

1. Identify the deepest fear you have related to some of the negative emotions you sometimes experience.

2. Identify the attachment longing related to the fear and articulate it verbally.

3. Turn this information into an explicit reaching out to your partner to give them the chance to respond.

To reiterate, here are some benefits to creating positive emotional bonding conversations:

- When you label your deepest fear, you have more ability to regulate the emotion.

- If you are clear when you emotionally reach out, you give your partner more ability to respond.

- You set yourself up for the benefits of effective dependence referred to earlier, wherein the more confident you are that you can reach your partner, the more autonomously you can function.

- By generating positive bonding, you build security into the relationship to inoculate against stressors that wear people down.

- This type of conversation contains the elements of accessibility, responsiveness, and engagement (A.R.E.) that reinforce couple attachment.

ANSON AND DANIELLE:
JOINT FEARS AND NEEDS

Anson grew up as the youngest child in a large, overachieving, politically visible family. His four older brothers and two sisters set a precedent of achievement, securing the public image their parents wanted to project. However, Anson struggled more in school than his older siblings. His parents hired tutors to help, but he had a sense that he wasn't measuring up to his siblings, and he worried about being a disappointment to his parents.

Fast-forward to Anson being married with four children. He and his wife disagreed about parenting their children. Danielle thought Anson had unrealistic expectations, and if she saw him being too hard on the children, she would step in and criticize him for his actions. He would then feel unsupported and alone, not unlike the feelings he carried as a child in his family.

As he and Danielle pondered about what their deepest fears were, Anson struggled at first to identify any fear. He finally said that he felt "frustrated" and "judged" by his wife. As I questioned him about other possible emotions he might feel when he felt criticized by Danielle, he did mention that he was "hurt" that she thought he was unreasonable, when he only wanted what was best for the children. He also came up with "shame," and said that he did have some of the feelings he had when he was a child, worrying that he just couldn't figure things out because he was flawed somehow. He also said he worried that he didn't have the ability to parent, so he also experienced a type of parental shame in which his children's behaviors directly impacted his feelings of self-worth.

Anson struggled to identify a deeper fear, which was no surprise. Like most men, he had been socialized not to acknowledge a "weak" emotion like fear. He learned to suppress or dismiss those feelings, which would usually resurface as annoyance. However, he stuck with it, and when I asked him what he was very anxious about, since anxiety is a form of fear, he finally said, "That I'm not enough. I don't have what it takes to be a successful husband and father, and person, for that matter. My wife will figure out that I'm not that great, and she will leave me. Then, I'll be a total failure." As he spoke these words out loud, he began rubbing his eyes to manage the emotions rising to the surface.

I turned to his wife and asked what happened for her as she saw her husband express his deepest fears. She had already reached out and put her hand on his arm to comfort him. She answered, "I had no idea. I just thought he was a rude jerk and mad all the time because he wanted to control his children the way his parents tried to control him, and he thought I was dumb because I thought he was being too harsh." She told Anson that it was helpful for her to know that he really had these core fears, because she didn't want him to have to worry about whether he was enough for her.

The next step for Anson, besides identifying his biggest fear, was to identify an attachment longing. Here are some common ones identified by Sue Johnson in her book *Hold Me Tight,* and some that come up in therapy:

- I need to know that I matter to you.
- I need to know that you still love me even if I'm not perfect.
- I need to know that you see my efforts, even if I don't get it right all the time.
- I need to know that you value me and will come close if I need you.
- I need to know that you value our partnership and want to work on us.
- I need to know that I am special to you.

When I talked to Anson about possible attachment longings, he articulated his need for acceptance for his sincere efforts. He clarified, "I need to know that you see me trying to slow down and be less reactive with the children, and that you can support me while I am figuring out how to be less reactive as a father. I need to know that you see me fundamentally as a good person despite my mistakes."

His wife spontaneously reached over to hug him and said, "Of course I see you as a good person. I lose my temper, too. I don't expect you to be perfect all the time. When you can tell me what's really going on, I understand you better and can help you. We both need help from each other."

In her part of the conversation, she revealed that she also had a deep fear related to her negative feelings of hurt and sadness in the marriage. She explained to Anson that she had some of the same fears he described. She said, "I worry that I'm not really the person you wanted. You wanted someone who could play the role your mother played, and you wish you were with someone different. I drag you down." As we worked on what she needed in the relationship, she clarified that she needed to know that he still loved her and wanted to work with her even if she disagreed with him sometimes about the best way to parent. When she clarified this, he reassured her, and they were both able to see by identifying their fears that they had a lot in common.

The cycle diagram on page 88 shows how verbalizing fears and emotional needs keeps the couple from stepping into their cycle and/or how it can help them step out:

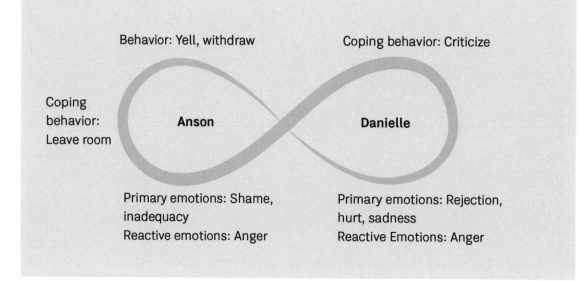

Behavior: Yell, withdraw

Coping behavior: Criticize

Coping behavior: Leave room

Anson

Danielle

Primary emotions: Shame, inadequacy
Reactive emotions: Anger

Primary emotions: Rejection, hurt, sadness
Reactive Emotions: Anger

Assessing Your Needs for Reassurance

Read the following common needs for reassurance or comfort and check the ones that apply to you. See if you can think of any others and write them on the lines that follow.

☐ I need to know that I matter to you.

☐ I need to know that you still love me even if I'm not perfect.

☐ I need to know that you see my efforts, even if I don't get it right all the time.

☐ I need to know that you value me and will come close if I need you.

☐ I need to be reminded about what you still love about me.

☐ I need to know that you value our partnership and want to work on us.

☐ I need to know that I am special to you.

☐ I just need to know that you can reach out and hold my hand.

☐ I just need a hug for comfort.

....

....

....

....

....

....

....

....

....

....

Reflecting on Reassurance

Sometimes sharing fears and needs can be incredibly anxiety-producing. Answer these questions to think about taking that risk. Interestingly, you might find that you need reassurance to feel comfortable asking for reassurance.

What feels risky about sharing my fears with my partner?

....

....

What would it be like to reach out with an emotional need?

....

....

What other experiences have I had with sharing my fears?

....

....

What other experiences have I had with telling people what I need?

....

....

Remember, sometimes it helps to think in parts. See if you can complete this sentence:

Part of me can see the benefit of sharing, but part of me is afraid that if I did share my fears and emotional needs, then

....

....

....

....

The most catastrophic thing that could happen if I shared this part of myself would be

....

....

....

....

....

In order to share this with my partner, I would need reassurance that

....

....

....

....

....

Behavior: Yell, withdraw   Coping behavior: Criticize

Coping
behavior:
Leave room   **Anson**   **Danielle**

Primary emotions: Shame,   Primary emotions: Rejection,
inadequacy   hurt, sadness
Reactive emotions: Anger   Reactive Emotions: Anger

Linking Emotions to Attachment Fears

John Bowlby posited that our attachment systems are active throughout our lifetimes and that humans naturally experience fear when their attachment figures are unresponsive or unavailable. He also asserted that humans prepare for fear contingencies. We scan our environments continually to try to predict attachment outcomes. If the alarm bell of disconnection is triggered in an argument, however, people don't realize that their negative emotions can likely be linked to attachment fears. Identifying attachment fears can take practice, but I haven't met a couple yet who couldn't connect distressing emotions to a baseline fear. In EFT, Sue Johnson suggests that when couples can identify their deepest fears, they can more easily link those fears to attachment longings and needs.

> *When couples can identify their deepest fears, they can more easily link those fears to attachment longings and needs.*

I adapted an activity originally created by Sue Johnson for her *Hold Me Tight* couples' workshops. This process helps couples distill their emotional needs so they can reach out to each other more clearly. Think of the last argument you had with your partner. Circle which of these words fit some of the emotions you were feeling:

Abandoned	Demeaned	Humiliated	Panicky
Accused	Despair	Hurt	Powerless
Alienated	Disappointed	Inadequate	Rejected
Alone	Dumb	Incompetent	Small
Angry	Embarrassed	Insecure	Terrified
Anxious	Empty	Insignificant	Timid
Ashamed	Failure	Invisible	Unaccepted
Attacked	Foolish	Irritated	Unloved
Belittled	Frustrated	Lonely	Unsafe
Betrayed	Guilty	Lost	Unwanted
Confused	Helpless	Misunderstood	Vulnerable
Criticized	Hopeless	Numb	Worthless

Any emotions that were not included on the list:

....

....

....

If you think about it, there is almost always some type of catastrophic fear that can be identified that relates to the negative emotion. In EFT, the image of taking an escalator down sometimes helps people think about their baseline fears.

Here are some common ones:

1. I get afraid that I'll never be enough

2. I get afraid that you will leave

3. I get afraid that I will always be alone

4. I get afraid that in the end I will have failed

5. I get afraid that there's something fundamentally wrong with me

Can you take the escalator down and link baseline fears to uncomfortable emotions?

When I feel these feelings (top of escalator), I realize that I get afraid that (bottom of escalator):

When I am feeling this way, I need reassurance or comfort that:

....

....

Can you share this information with your partner?

....

....

....

THE ROLE OF RESPONDING

The flip side of reaching out to a partner is responding and engaging with a partner. Sometimes, partners worry that if they are responsive, they are building in emotional dependence, so they will purposely withhold and/or ration their emotional responsiveness. However, research confirms that people with more responsive partners function more autonomously. In the **dependency paradox**, people who can't predict that partners will respond will develop more anxious "clinginess," that can feel suffocating. People who feel secure in the knowledge that they can reach out and gain emotional responsiveness tend to function more autonomously. Partner responsiveness is the foundation for secure attachment. When partners show a lack of emotional responsiveness, they also diminish the security that is foundational to independence.

When Your Emotional Need Triggers Your Partner's Emotional Need

Sometimes, I've noticed that reaching out with an emotional need might bump up against the other partner's emotional need. For instance, if one partner questions their own ability to comfort or reassure the other partner, they might be more tentative about moving in close to offer support. When people worry that their offers for reassurance and/or comfort will be rejected, they tend to be more tentative about responding. Sometimes those partners need reassurance that their presence is having a positive impact.

Here's an example. When Shane saw his wife crying and tried to comfort her, he thought that he was unsuccessful because she was still crying. His fear of inadequacy was triggered. When she explained that it was helpful to have him come close, even if she was still sad, "because then at least I'm not sad alone," he had more confidence that he was still effective, even if she was still displaying distress.

Answer these questions to explore your responses to emotional need:

1. What have you learned about responding to emotional need in relationships?

2. What might prevent you from wanting to reassure or comfort your partner?

3. What reassurance do you need to make it easier to respond to your partner's emotional need?

Maintaining Connection to Facilitate Emotional Bonding

I have found that the more couples take charge of and prioritize their connection, the more likely they are to maintain enough safety to share fears and reach out to have their emotional needs met. I have observed that checking in on a connection can strengthen connection. It's a very simple process. Couples can do a daily, weekly, or monthly check-in. Structure it according to your schedule. Take a few minutes regularly to jointly answer these questions:

1. How connected do I feel to my partner compared to the last time we checked? (Circle one.)

   More   Less   Same

2. What has been happening in our relationship that may have contributed to the level of connection we have?

   ....

   ....

3. To feel more connected, one thing that would help is reassurance or comfort that:

   ....

   ....

   ....

TYING IT TOGETHER

Congratulations! You now know how to intentionally create positive bonding experiences in your cycle to strengthen connection. The next section addresses particularly painful events that can sometimes keep couples stuck.

Key points:

- Couples can learn to identify their emotions and needs and can reach out to create positive bonding when they aren't triggered in a cycle.

- These bonding conversations can help increase security to prevent rapid disconnection.

- To identify an emotional need, it helps to link negative emotion to a baseline fear.

- Once the fear is identified, it's easier to articulate what reassurance or comfort one needs.

- It helps to acknowledge that both partners might have needs and can both get reassurance.

- Couples can intentionally address their levels of connection to help maintain their connection.

CHAPTER SEVEN

Healing Attachment Injuries

In all bonded romantic relationships, forgiveness is a daily necessity and has a huge positive impact on couple happiness. There are different types of forgiveness. One is daily forgiveness for minor slights. The other type is sometimes harder to access, but is necessary for major offenses that erode overall trust. In EFT, these major offenses are called "attachment injuries" and must be addressed for the relationship to continue.

Forgiveness *never* means putting oneself in harm's way or tolerating ongoing, repetitive, serious harmful behavior, such as abuse, affairs, or addictions that compromise the safety of daily life. Forgiveness also doesn't mean forgetting offenses. We don't forget, but we learn to process and work through emotion to generate healing moments and rebuild trust amid the remembering.

WHAT ARE ATTACHMENT INJURIES?

In close relationships, couples are bound to injure each other. Forgiveness researcher and expert Dr. Frank Fincham asserts that if you are in a close long-term relationship, it is inevitable that you will be hurt along the way. We all have annoying habits that can become irritating to our partner over time, and no one escapes having to deal with these annoyances. Dr. John Gottman is famous for asserting that when you marry a person, you marry a set of problems. However, sometimes serious ruptures in trust will keep a couple disconnected indefinitely if they aren't specifically addressed.

A classic definition of an **attachment injury** is an intense trauma or "violation of trust that brings the nature of the whole relationship into question and must be dealt with if the relationship is to survive." One indicator that an attachment injury is present is when couples have learned to stop negative patterns, but still struggle to take any significant risks because of diminished trust. A big reason why these injuries require specific care is so partners can build a foundation of safety to support risk-taking. Here are some common characteristics of attachment injuries:

- Basic assumptions about the relationship are shattered. Suddenly, everything comes into question. What couples thought they knew for sure is nonexistent.

- There is a sense that the partner is a stranger.

- There is a sense of "never again" in which partners protect themselves so they won't feel that pain of betrayal again.

Exercising Forgiveness

Identify some of the minor slights you forgive your partner for on a daily basis:
Here are some common examples of minor injuries you might forgive regularly.
Check any that apply and then add your own:

☐ Leaving wet towels on the floor

☐ Leaving the almost-empty milk carton in the refrigerator

☐ Leaving clothes all over the bedroom

☐ Leaving dishes in the sink

☐ Leaving the gas tank empty

_____

_____

_____

_____

_____

_____

_____

_____

_____

Common Attachment Injuries

An attachment injury can be anything that diminishes safety to the extent described on page 100.

Common attachment injuries that regularly surface in therapy are:

- Financial betrayal or secrets (e.g., spending all the money in a joint bank account, the discovery of a secret bank account, opening up a credit card and accumulating debt affecting the partner, secretly sending money to a family member)

- Infidelity (e.g., an emotional or physical affair)

- Sudden emotional unavailability during a critical time (e.g., when losing a parent or child, when receiving a serious diagnosis or living with a serious illness)

- Hiding something significant (e.g., an abortion that took place without the other partner's knowledge, a substance abuse problem, a pornography habit, or something major from the past like a prison term or other children)

- Suddenly becoming physically abusive

A Note on Infidelity

Media presentations of infidelity often fail to capture the full range of emotional collateral damage it causes to the relationship. Besides deception, infidelity is a type of injury in which another person was essentially "chosen" over the partner. A partner shared a set of experiences exclusive to this other partnership, and the betrayed partner was not present in that shared space. In essence, their repeated questioning (which often accompanies the discovery of infidelity) is an attempt to establish presence in a space that was entirely unknown and where they were barred access. The intimate, shared nature of infidelity is possibly the most painful of attachment injuries, and can take longer than other injuries to heal.

Identifying Your Attachment Injuries

As you think about your relationship history, are there any defining moments that possibly put you on guard and made it harder to trust your partner?

If so, describe the incident here:

....

....

....

What emotions do you remember experiencing at the time?

....

....

What emotions come up right now as you think about it?

....

....

Have you had the chance to describe how painful or difficult this situation was for you?

....

What can your partner do to signal understanding of the depth of this experience?

....

....

What does your partner do that helps you feel safe in the present?

....

....

KIM AND SAM, PART I

Attachment injuries can come up at any time during therapy. Sometimes, couples aren't even aware that they still experience diminished trust and pain from past injuries.

Kim and Sam sought therapy for escalating arguments that were getting "out of control." They described three incidences of physical abuse a decade before in which Sam shoved Kim, but both said they had gone to therapy and stopped all physical violence. I felt comfortable meeting with them together since they had stopped the violence for a decade after three discrete instances, and separately reported no perceived threat of future physical altercations. Kim expressed some ambivalence about staying married at first, but once therapy began, she reported high motivation to decrease their arguments and stay together.

The couple progressed quickly, learning to slow down, identify their negative patterns, and step out of them. In fact, I was a little worried that change was happening a little too fast, because it seemed too good to be true. Even though Kim indicated a higher desire to stay in the marriage and engaged in therapy, Sam seemed uneasy and expressed that he couldn't really trust her because her pattern had been to immediately escalate into anger and threaten the marriage unpredictably. He reported that even though she was saying things were good now, it appeared to him that she could discard the marriage at the drop of a hat. He said any time he expressed sadness about losing the marriage, she just seemed "angry." He wasn't sure she really cared about him enough to stay.

I realized that we needed to explore some of the hurt that had been building up before she exploded in anger and threatened to leave. Although Kim had been softer in our sessions and expressed some sad emotions, Sam actually displayed more sadness and fear about the marriage ending while Kim showed more relief about their improvement. He wasn't sure if she was being honest about the situation. Since she didn't really express much emotion except anger, he was convinced that she wasn't as committed to the relationship as he. (More about this couple later.)

Addressing Attachment Injuries

There are specific steps for attaining forgiveness in the event of an attachment injury, which have been verified in EFT research. Sometimes couples think that if they avoid talking about the painful emotions, they will eventually die down and the couple will heal with time. That's not the case. I have literally seen couples who were disconnected for forty years because they never verbally discussed an attachment injury because the content made them both uncomfortable. All they did was get better at avoiding it and slowly grew more distant. Attachment injuries *must* be addressed specifically. Here are the main steps:

1. **Injured partner shares core emotions.** The important thing here is to express from the softer side of the pain rather than the protective anger, which does a good job of keeping people from getting too close too fast, but which also prevents offending partners from getting close enough to the pain to understand and validate it. The softer side is often the hurt, fear, and lack of safety from the event.

2. **Offending partner validates pain.** The partner can be curious about the softer pain. Asking about it non-defensively and validating it can genuinely help the injured partner start to organize their experience in a coherent narrative so they can move past it.

3. **Injured partner shares any deeper related emotions.** The next step is for injured partners to share at a deeper level, perhaps incorporating fears of being injured again.

4. **Offending partner offers genuine empathy.** The offending partner displays congruent emotion emanating from the shame of hearing about their partner's hurt, i.e., "I hurt that I made you hurt."

5. **Injured partner intentionally reaches out for support.** The hurt partner can reach out for the comfort and reassurance they need as they manage triggers moving forward.

6. **Offending partner continues to respond to the injured partner's outreach.** The offending partner offers reassurance and comfort in the present, displaying "I am here now."

7. **The couple together creates a narrative for the relationship moving forward.** For example, "Before, we were living with distance and managing crises that took our attention away from the relationship. Now, we are aware of the risks this poses to our connection, and we actively look for ways to reach out and offer comfort and reassurance to prevent future disconnection."

Barriers to Forgiveness

There are several reasons why couples struggle to heal these major injuries. Here are some that come up frequently:

- It is hard for partners who feel shame about having hurt their partner to stay present to hear their pain. The antidote is to disclose the feelings of shame and/or regret that make it painful to hear, while staying present.

- Healing takes a long time. It may seem strange, but it's important to not "heal" too quickly. Time is an important variable for healing, even when paired with consistent empathic responses. I usually tell people that, for example, in the case of an affair, two years is not a long time. Regardless, they will always want it to be faster. Hurt partners tire of feeling emotional pain, and offending partners tire of hearing repetitive rehearsals of pain. That's a normal part of the process. In fact, if partners trust too quickly, that might mean they aren't being genuine in their responses.

- Healing is almost always nonlinear. This is important, because if couples are feeling better but then get triggered into painful emotion, they might think they aren't making progress. I remind couples that healing is up-and-down with the goal being an overall upward trajectory over time.

- The need for repeated reassurance can be daunting to offending partners, but repeated, consistent reassurance is one of the few ways people can gain confidence that the injury won't be repeated. It is soothing to ask for information and receive consistent responses. Defensiveness, however, is alarming. Sometimes, offending partners need to be reminded that repetition is okay. If a partner asks the same question 100 times, then getting the same answer 100 times is more reassuring than getting the same answer 99 times, and then getting a defensive, "WHY DO YOU KEEP ASKING? I DON'T HAVE A DIFFERENT ANSWER!" one time.

- It is disorienting to get healing from someone who hurt you, so attachment becomes predictably disorganized. Injured people will seek closeness with a partner and then get scared or upset and push the partner away. Some therapists (usually those who are overwhelmed by the process themselves) will unwittingly and inaccurately label this behavior borderline personality disorder, when the behavior is actually normative and expected for a relationship trauma.

- Ambivalence is the norm. Injured partners will equivocate between wanting to work on the relationship and wanting distance, which can be confusing.

- The emotional range is all over the board, easily overwhelming both partners. Emotions related to attachment injuries are notoriously high and need constant validation. There really are no limits to the emotion that can arise from attachment injuries.

- Partners need a combination of time and information to make sense of the injury. They need time to grieve the loss of the relationship they thought they had and to create a narrative for a new relationship.

- It's normal to develop extra sensitivity to deception. Deception is the main damaging component behind attachment injuries. It's difficult to attach safely to what you don't feel you can trust. I tell partners, "If you say you're going to turn right, and you turn left, you can trigger a partner." Honesty and predictability absolutely must be visible to rebuild any kind of safety. One lie can take an injured partner right back to the starting line.

Reflection Questions

Thinking about our relationship, has trust been compromised in a big rupture? If so, how?

....

....

....

Does the rupture trigger emotions from earlier life experiences? If so, what?

....

....

....

What have we done to try to heal this rupture?

....

....

....

What emotions have been closest to the surface for me?

....

....

....

What emotions have been closest to the surface for my partner?

....

....

....

In my opinion, the thing that keeps us the most stuck is:

....

....

....

Are there any ways the relationship feels more supportive than before? (For example, going to therapy or even filling out a workbook is a step toward healing. So is articulating boundaries differently, or describing how a partner now helps with caretaking a relationship when they weren't intentionally doing so before.)

....

....

....

One thing that I really need my partner to understand so I can move forward is:

....

....

....

One thing that can increase safety in the relationship right now is:

....

....

....

KIM AND SAM,
PART II: PROCESSING INJURIES

I asked Kim if she could describe the pain that was building up before she left her husband and threatened divorce. Instead of speaking, she began shaking her head and was visibly struggling with language. I asked for help to understand what was happening. She finally explained, "I promised myself a decade ago when he shoved me that I would never be vulnerable with him again." I suddenly remembered the three incidents of physical abuse that they claimed had been resolved. This made me certain that I was dealing with a lingering attachment injury. I asked whether they had ever processed the events verbally, and they said they had never talked about it. The abuse stopped, but they never went back to the therapist and discussed it, nor did they talk about it with each other.

I asked Kim what was coming up as she was thinking about it in the moment. She started to describe the events of physical violence that had been terrifying to her, especially since Sam had a much larger stature. She began sobbing as much as I have seen anyone sob, shoulders shaking and voice gasping. I saw an opportunity for them to heal the injury from the past in a way they hadn't before, since the emotion was so real.

I asked Sam about the feelings that were coming up for him, and he expressed a great deal of shame and regret, as well as hopelessness because he couldn't change the events of the past. I asked if he could describe those feelings to her directly, and he turned to her and explained more about what he told me. His sorrowful manner stayed congruent with his language, so it seemed trustworthy to her.

After Sam expressed the impact her pain was having on him, she spontaneously turned toward him and told him that she knew sometimes people lose their temper, and she also knew he was trying to be different in the present. For the first time in ten years, Kim could express the deep emotional impact and lack of safety she experienced back then, and Sam was able to hear her pain and express sorrow and compassion. This was a key moment in therapy and it helped them gain more trust in each other.

Healing Options

From what you have learned, can you circle the option that might help both partners heal?

1. You had a great weekend with your partner. It was the first time in three months that they didn't bring up the affair you disclosed. You finally think you're on a path to healing. Suddenly, while you're getting ready for work on Monday morning, you find your partner crying, looking at a photo album and remembering the relationship before the affair. You immediately feel discouraged about the progress you made. How can you respond to manage the emotions in this situation?

   a. Why do you have to ruin a perfectly good weekend by bringing up the past?

   b. I'm so sorry that the pain is coming up again (with eye contact). When you bring it up, I start worrying that I can't help you heal. I know I put our relationship at risk, but I do want to help you feel better. What do you need me to understand right now?

   c. Oh my gosh! It wasn't even a real affair. It's not like I had sex with her or anything—we just talked and shared feelings and made out a few times. Do you know how many people I know who have had sexual affairs?

2. Your partner is leaving town for the first time since you found out they were secretly going to bars and drinking when they were out of town after claiming sobriety after having undergone rehab following a DUI. So far, you have been going to therapy and they have been more transparent about sensitive feelings and urges, but you are feeling unsafe and panicky that they might betray your trust again. How can you articulate your feelings in a way your partner can give you reassurance?

   a. Use a snarky tone to say, "Call me while you're still sober."

   b. Try to suppress your feelings and become generally irritable instead.

   c. Say, "I'm getting that uncertain feeling about you leaving town. Can you remind me how you see our relationship differently than before, so I know you aren't building resentment toward me when I ask for reassurance that you're staying sober?"

3. Your partner lied to you about having an emotional affair with your best friend. They keep trying to reassure you, but you are struggling to feel any kind of emotional safety. Which choice might help you elicit the type of comfort and reassurance you would need?

   a. Why don't you just go text the slut?

   b. I am having a hard time feeling any peace. Can you explain how you are caretaking the boundaries of our relationship differently than before?

   c. All you ever think about is yourself. You are the most selfish human being ever!

THINGS WERE GOING SO WELL . . .

It's very common that even when healing does start to happen, hurt partners can revert to a panicky, anxious, angry stance, which is confusing and discouraging to the offending partner. It's almost always a way to express pain and fear of pain. Sometimes, I help the hurt partner clarify their emotional shifts verbally. It's common to be afraid that if things heal too fast, a partner might think that they are all better. The partner might just move on and forget how painful this was for the injured partner, and get careless about the relationship. The reaction is a version of, "I need you to know that this was painful enough that I'm still healing, and I can't imagine going through this pain again."

The #1 Thing I Wish More Offending Partners Would Do

Offending partners really struggle with their own emotional reactivities and with the shame of causing their partner pain. They can feel hopeless and afraid that their partner's expression of pain is a sign that they might decide to leave them. As a result, they end up trying to avoid conversations in which the injured partner talks about their pain. However, by asking about a partner's pain, an offending partner signals that they care and want to understand the pain, and that they want to offer healing. I'm convinced that if I could get more partners to ask, "How is your pain from the injury in our relationship?" they could soothe their partners faster.

I created a "pain check-in" questionnaire that I will sometimes give to people as a way to feel safer inquiring about a partner's pain. It consists of just a few questions:

Where is your emotional pain level today on a scale of 1 to 10?

Is there anything right now that you need me to understand?

Is there anything that might help alleviate the pain just one degree?

I'm not expecting partners to just immediately feel all better, but I am hoping that partners can gain more comfort inviting discussion about the injury, because it benefits both partners.

TYING IT TOGETHER

Injuries can be healed, but not if both partners are too afraid to address them directly. If needed, consult a therapist to help facilitate a direct conversation. My experience with couples is that therapy can make a profound difference.

Key points:

- Forgiveness is a key ingredient in couple happiness.

- Attachment injuries are severe violations of trust that compromise the safety of the entire relationship.

- Attachment injuries can create the sense that one's partner is a stranger.

- Attachment injuries can keep a couple disconnected if not addressed directly.

- There is a template to guide couples through talking about attachment injuries.

- Infidelity is usually an especially painful type of attachment injury.

- Partners can invite a lot of healing by voluntarily asking about the pain from the attachment injury.

PART THREE

Strengthening Connections

One mistake couples sometimes make is that they will improve in therapy and then decide they have enough tools to create emotional bonding on their own. However, they then stop putting in the same effort they were exerting while they were in counseling, and so they begin to drift. Additionally, some couples might feel more connected, but still avoid dealing with sexual intimacy because they don't always understand how to apply the principles of healing in their sexual relationship. The chapters in part 3 will focus on strengthening the sexual relationship as well as nourishing the relationship with increased intentionality.

CHAPTER EIGHT

• • • •

Maintaining Intimacy

I took my first sex therapy class in graduate school in the late 1980s. I had little to no discomfort discussing sexual issues, so I was certain I would have all the answers to treat couples' sexual dilemmas in therapy. Unfortunately, despite my sex-positive attitude, I learned that couple sexuality is a complex, multifaceted, ever-evolving, and vulnerable area between couples. I was going to have to step back, increase my patience as well as my knowledge base, and honor the nuances that arise in couples' sexual relationships.

I have learned that when it comes to sexuality, emotional safety is often preeminent. Minority populations who don't identify with a heterosexual majority might need special care because they have often developed shame from rejection or had traumatic experiences while developing sexual identities. Whenever addressing sexual issues, I work very hard at emotionally attuning to the couples to help them formulate their own process of increasing their mutual responsiveness and discovering a pathway to a mutually satisfying sexual relationship.

In a large majority of my relationship therapy cases, if sex does not come up as a problem area in the first few sessions, it will eventually come up later. That's because there is such a high correlation between general relationship happiness and sexual satisfaction. I view sex as a sort of litmus test that will eventually reflect the challenges in the overall relationship. Emotional intimacy and sexual intimacy seem to reciprocally influence each other in long-term romantic bonds. Sexual engagement usually becomes part of the couple's negative cycle, particularly in the common case of differences in sex desire.

FINDING INTIMACY

Sexuality is a central component of adult romantic attachment bonds. Sex researcher Dr. Barry McCarthy found that in a good relationship, about 15 to 20 percent of the relationship was attributed to the sexual relationship, and that in a poor-quality relationship, 50 to 70 percent of the distress was attributed to sex, illustrating how sex is generally an important area of negotiation in any long-term relationship. Research also indicates that great sex doesn't happen by accident; couples who report high-quality sex also prioritize this part of their union. When couples understand its place in the attachment system and learn to cultivate safety and authentic empathy, they set the groundwork for positive sexual relationships.

There are many reasons couples have sex in long-term relationships, such as reassurance, recreation, reproduction, expressing affection, bonding, and stress management. In fact, sex is associated with several physical health benefits, and it prompts our body to release oxytocin, a hormone believed to play a part in couple bonding.

Sex is considered part of the adult romantic attachment system. The anxious and avoidant tendencies that show up in insecure relationships will commonly play out in the sexual relationship. Thus, anxious partners can seem aggressive, coercive, and demanding about wanting sex, or they may rigidly require a certain level of emotional connection before sex, which compromises security in the other partner. Avoidant partners can seem emotionally disconnected during sex, or sex might be the only form of closeness they pursue in the relationship regardless of emotional connection. Both scenarios can compromise a sense of safety and comfort when it comes to sex.

Since sex is a form of exploration and play in a relationship, secure attachment is often necessary for both partners to feel comfort with sexual risk-taking. Sexual arousal is also fostered in an environment of low anxiety, where individuals feel accepted. Any attachment distress will often hinder individual and couple sexual activity and quality, and can exacerbate conditions like erectile dysfunction and/or any sexual pain disorders. Conflict introduces insecurity in partners, so when couples are stuck in negative patterns, sex is highly likely to be compromised.

Dr. Sue Johnson conceptualizes three sexual styles in couples, directly related to attachment: Sealed-off sex, solace sex, and synchrony sex. **Sealed-off sex** is characterized by a focus on "sensation and performance," devoid of emotional connection, and shows up often as a strategy used by avoidant individuals. It is essentially a detached approach. **Solace sex** is the term used to describe the pattern of anxious individuals seeking soothing primarily through sexual activity, particularly if they can't get reassurance about their worth through emotional means. **Synchrony sex** is the term used to describe mutual risk-taking, openness, and responsiveness in an exchange where couples can bring their complete selves to the sexual relationship without fear of being judged or criticized. They can risk-take without fear of rejection and in turn attune to their partners to communicate loving acceptance.

PEAK SEXUAL EXPERIENCES

There's no question that we live in a sex-centric society where we are bombarded by messages for how to have "The. Best. Sex. Ever." Many of the messages offer advice in the way of positions, techniques, toys, and other mechanistic features of sex. Dr. Peggy Kleinplatz and her colleagues studied what couples really report as far as peak sexual experiences, and they released the findings in their book *Magnificent Sex*. They found that regardless of sexual orientation, most people report that their peak experiences are related to elements of sexual accessibility, responsiveness, and engagement. These elements are all alluded to in synchrony sex and in overall adult attachment processes. Despite messages in the media, people don't generally tie their peak experiences to new techniques, but to relationships in which they can safely explore sexual desires and eroticism in a safe, nonjudgmental, empathic environment. In fact, empathy came up repeatedly among research respondents as the main ingredient for great sex. In long-term relationships, couples benefit from accepting the reality that sexual satisfaction naturally waxes and wanes. The acceptance of less-than-ideal sex can ease anxieties to make room for future positive sexual encounters.

> *Despite messages in the media, people don't generally tie their peak experiences to new techniques, but to relationships in which they can safely explore sexual desires and eroticism in a safe, nonjudgmental, empathic environment.*

Identifying Sexual Styles and Attachment

Read each of the following scenarios and see if you can recognize the type of sex described in each situation:

1. Rachel grew up in what she called a "hypersexual environment," where her parents frequently brought multiple sex partners into the home and engaged in sexual activities freely in front of the children. They were also negligent about childcare and would leave and sometimes not come home all night. Rachel explained that if her husband didn't want to have sex, she would "panic" and feel anxious about her worth to him until they had sex again. Rachel is displaying elements of:

    Synchrony Sex   Solace Sex   Sealed-Off Sex

2. Adi grew up gay in a conservative religious environment where he felt "broken and bad" for his attraction to members of the same sex. He described wanting to be able to combine sexual and emotional closeness, but he struggled to feel emotionally vulnerable while engaging sexually. He described feeling "emotionally numb" while having sex, and said he was primarily focused on physical sensations. Adi is displaying elements of:

    Synchrony Sex   Solace Sex   Sealed-Off Sex

3. Claudia told her partner Darius about a sexual trauma she had experienced. When he offered real understanding, validating her fears and communicating to her that he wanted her to feel safe during their sexual relationship, she took more risks to tell him what she preferred during sex. Eventually, she described being able to engage without monitoring herself and having the ability to nonverbally attune to Darius, because she wasn't worried about what he was thinking. This scenario is an example of:

    Synchrony Sex   Solace Sex   Sealed-Off Sex

Answers are: 1. Solace Sex, 2. Sealed-Off Sex, 3. Synchrony Sex

ANTOINE AND MARJORIE IN A PURSUE-WITHDRAW PATTERN OF SEX

Antoine and Marjorie had been living together for three years when they came in. They described their early sexual relationship as "organic, easy, and mutually satisfying." They said they didn't really have to "overthink it" because they both felt accepted, and it seemed to grow out of their relationship.

However, as they developed negative patterns typical of a pursue-withdraw pattern, they simultaneously seemed to develop a large sexual desire discrepancy in which Antoine reported higher desire and consistently wanted sex more often than Marjorie. Marjorie complained that the "only way Antoine wants to connect now is by having sex." She explained, "He'll be mean to me all day and then want to have sex that night, which just blows me away. How am I supposed to have sex with someone that has been rejecting me all day? That's basically prostitution." At times, she would force herself to have sex with him just to "keep him happy," but then she developed more resentment and negativity about having sex.

Antoine's complaint was that he was "expected to be perfect" before Marjorie would consider having sex with him. "It doesn't matter what happens during the day. I can be the most attentive male on earth and she will still find an excuse to avoid having sex with me." He proceeded to describe the deep feelings of rejection he experienced daily, "Most of the time when we do have sex, she seems totally disengaged and I end up feeling like a rapist, which I hate. That's a terrible feeling." He was convinced that she must not be physically attracted to him, or that he was somehow flawed in his sexual technique. "Maybe I'm just bad at sex," he lamented.

Reaching out sexually for him was a way to gain reassurance and comfort that he was loved, but for Marjorie, engaging sexually was difficult without the emotional reassurance for the security to know that she was more than just an object for his release. The more he felt hopeless about meeting her emotional needs, the more he avoided contact with her so he wouldn't "get it wrong and make things worse." He wasn't practiced at putting his emotional needs into words, so Marjorie didn't believe that sex was an emotional connection for him. She saw him as just wanting "orgasm." The more he reached out for sex for his own reassurance, the more she withdrew from engaging until she had more emotional safety. Thus, their mutuality in feeling stuck in their negative pattern was reinforced at both the sexual and emotional level.

Attachment Cycles and Sex

In your current relationship, is there a partner who reaches out more often for sex? If so, who?

To be filled out by the partner who reaches out more for sex: Answer the following questions, keeping in mind where they occur in the cycle.

1. When I reach out for sex, my partner reacts to me by:

   ....

   ....

2. When my partner reacts this way, I feel:

   ....

   ....

3. When my partner reacts this way, this is what I say to myself about our sexual relationship:

   ....

   ....

4. Then, I end up coping by:

   ....

   ....

5. Then, I'm guessing my partner feels:

....

....

6. What my partner says to themselves is:

....

....

7. Then, they cope by:

....

....

8. Can you put into words any reassurance/comfort you get from having sex?

....

....

For the partner who reaches out less or is approached more for sex: Answer the following questions, keeping in mind where they occur in the cycle.

1. My partner reaches out to me for sex by:

....

....

2. When my partner reaches out this way, I feel:

   ....

   ....

3. When I feel this way, this is what I say to myself about our sexual relationship:

   ....

   ....

4. I cope with these feelings by:

   ....

   ....

5. When I cope this way, my partner probably feels:

   ....

   ....

6. Then, my partner says to themself:

   ....

   ....

7. Then they cope by:

   ....

   ....

8. Can you put into words the reassurance/comfort you might need to feel safe enough to engage sexually?

   ....

   ....

DEEPENING INTIMACY

What exactly is "sex" anyway? For years, the sex therapy field has identified the problems inherent in equating "sex" with orgasm. Early models of sexual response incorporated orgasm as an end goal, but there are many sexual interactions independent of orgasm that may or may not lead to orgasm. Dr. Kleinplatz and her colleagues also found that couples didn't necessarily equate their optimal sexual experiences with orgasm. They pointed out that sex was overall associated with a "mind" exercise. Many activities can be perceived as sexual. In particular, they asserted that kissing was frequently viewed as an erotic exchange. When couples focus too heavily on orgasm, it can have a negative effect on the sexual relationship. Focusing on orgasm can increase anxiety about performance, which is a paradoxical barrier to sexual engagement. Focusing on orgasm as an outcome prevents people from being fully present in their sexual activities.

Couples also sometimes underestimate the power of warm, supportive touch for physical connection. Dr. Julianne Holt-Lundstad and colleagues found that increasing intentional warm touch between couples reduced stress. Since increased stress negatively impacts empathy, and empathy is a key ingredient for good sex, it's likely that couples who recognize the power of this kind of activity will lay the groundwork for better sex.

Besides setting aside time for intentional warm touch, couples can increase safety by disclosing beliefs and emotions around sex in an accepting environment. To share experiences and to feel understood allows for risk-taking and vulnerability in sexual communication and behavior. I commonly give couples a series of questions related to sex just to invite a conversation. The main guidelines for this type of conversation are that partners must be able to have their own opinions and emotions. When reviewing questions, partners can watch for their own emotional responses and practice deep breathing to stay regulated. Also, identifying the emotional reactions and fears that make them feel vulnerable can help regulate any reactivity.

Increase Comfort During Sex

Practice increasing understanding by sharing answers to any of these questions. You don't need to do them all at once. Pick just one or a few to discuss to increase comfort talking about sexuality:

1. When I think about sex, I: ....

2. Sex and love are: ....

3. Sex and emotion are: ....

4. My first sexual memory is: ....

5. Negative messages I received about sex while growing up are: ....

   ....

6. Positive messages I received about sex while growing up are: ....

   ....

7. The best part about sex is: ....

8. The scariest part about sex is: ....

9. The most difficult part about sex is: ....

10. The things that make it safer to engage sexually are: ....

11. I associate the sexual part of myself with: ....

12. One thing I would like to have more of in our sexual relationship is: ....

    ....

13. I feel most understood when: ....

    ....

14. When my partner touches me, I feel: ....

15. When I touch my partner, I feel: ....

16. When my partner sees me naked, I feel: ....

    ....

17. When I see my partner naked, I feel: ....

18. Before sex, I feel: _____

19. After sex, I feel: _____

20. I felt safe engaging sexually when: _____

_____

21. My best sexual experience with you was: _____

_____

_____

22. Sex is an expression of: _____

23. The sexual part of myself is: _____

24. I become sexually aroused when: _____

_____

25. Sexually, I like it when my partner: _____

_____

26. One time I felt comfortable having sex was: _____

_____

27. When it comes to our sexual relationship, I really need my partner to

understand: _____

_____

28. One thing I would like to try sexually is: _____

_____

29. One thing I like about my sexuality is: _____

_____

30. One thing that increases my desire for sex is: _____

Practicing Warm Touch

In the following table of various types of warm couple engagement, mark the behaviors you would like to try. Choose behaviors that you can risk-take authentically without forcing yourself. If you do risk-take with any behaviors, write down any results you noticed as a follow-up.

	I want to try:	Impact on me after trying:	Impact on my partner after trying:	Impact on our relationship:
Intentionally smiling at my partner to communicate affection:				
Greeting my partner with a kiss:				
Holding hands:				
Offering a hand massage:				
Touching nose to nose:				
Snuggling:				
Hugging for at least a minute:				
Complimenting my partner to communicate authentic warmth:				
Kissing for five minutes or longer:				

	I want to try:	Impact on me after trying:	Impact on my partner after trying:	Impact on our relationship:
Making eye contact with my partner for one minute:				
Giving my partner a shoulder rub:				
Giving my partner a back rub:				
Giving my partner a foot rub:				
Sitting across from each other and coordinate our breathing for at least two minutes:				
Touching my partner on the arm to communicate affection:				
Playing footsie with my partner:				
Slow dancing with my partner for five minutes:				

REPAIRING INTIMACY

Unfortunately, when people have negative experiences with sex, they tend to become more avoidant or anxious about having sex the next time. Sometimes previous sexual trauma might create emotional triggers. It can be helpful to slow down and have people use language to describe some of the emotional triggers along with what they need to find safety to continue. For serious trauma, individual therapy can be pursued along with or before couple's work.

Sometimes injuries can occur from competing sexual attachments in the relationship. These can be significant attachment injuries as discussed in the previous chapter that require special attention. A classic example is hidden pornography use. While some couples openly use pornography, many individuals feel betrayed by a partner's pornography use, and it can decrease sexual safety and increase relationship trauma. It's not uncommon for partners to have increased anxiety during sex after finding out that their partners have used pornography. They may wonder what their partners have been viewing and if they measure up. Sometimes it helps to identify what has been difficult about sex in the past to identify ways to rebuild safety and allow for vulnerability and risk-taking.

Reaching out for Reassurance and Safety

These are conversation starters to understand pain and learn to reach out for reassurance and safety:

1. My biggest fear about our sexual relationship is: _____

2. I would feel safer if I knew you understood: _____

3. I need reassurance that if I engage sexually with you, then: _____

4. Other types of engagement that would help me feel safer to engage

    sexually are: _____

Revisiting Antoine and Marjorie, this couple had a deeper, mutually empathic conversation during therapy that improved their sexual relationship. First, Antoine took more time to identify the emotional reassurance he derived from Marjorie's willingness to have sex with him. Instead of relying on solely reaching out to her for sex, he learned to put his insecurities into words so that Marjorie could see that he needed her for more than just physical release. She could see that he did care what she thought of him, and that sometimes he needed reassurance that he was physically desirable and was loved. When he learned the language to express some of these longings, Marjorie took more risks to explain her own fears that she didn't really matter to him and that he was using her as an object. She also worried about her own diminishing sexual desire and expressed the need for Antoine to slow down and attune to her so she could risk-take and become more present during sexual activity. They discussed their deep longings together, creating mutual understanding that led to mutual attunement in their lovemaking.

TYING IT TOGETHER

Sexual intimacy is one of the most compelling human experiences, and can reinforce bonding and safety when used carefully and intentionally for mutual benefit. Couples can heal rifts and increase emotional safety by acknowledging the ways in which sex is important to most romantic bonds but can also be a point of vulnerability. They can then work together to make sexual intimacy safe enough to explore and to take risks together.

Key points:

- A couple's long-term sexual relationship is complex, influenced by many variables, and continually being shaped.

- The sexual system is part of the adult attachment system.

- The sexual system and emotional system in the relationship usually reciprocally influence each other.

- Great sex doesn't happen naturally—couples need to work at it.

- Couples report that their optimal sexual experiences are not necessarily linked to orgasm, but rather to a high degree of presence and empathy.

- Warm, nonsexual physical touch can have a positive impact on couples.

- When couples can share their deeper feelings and elicit empathy, they are more likely to feel safe within their sexual relationship.

- Safety in the relationship often leads to more exploration and risk-taking in the sexual relationship.

CHAPTER NINE

• • •

Maintaining Bonds

It is inevitable that after a couple has managed to shift their negative patterns, they will ask, "Now, how do we avoid falling back into those old habits that brought us here in the first place?" This is a wise question, because couples who are not actively attending to their relationship quality are subject to a concept of "drift," meaning that there is a tendency for couples to become out of sync and disconnected over time unless something is done to prevent it. Relationships are always being shaped, like it or not. Couples who prevail against the infinite stressors inside and outside the bond are those who intentionally devise strategies for working on maintaining and protecting the relationship.

Anyone invested in a long-term romantic relationship and paying attention to media messages might feel hopeless that they can maintain love over time. Dr. William Doherty wrote that "the biggest threat to good marriages is everyday living," alluding to the various responsibilities that pull couples in various directions, fragmenting the relationship. His book *Take Back Your Marriage* emphasizes the power that couples possess to preserve their bonds when they put intentional practices into place.

We know more than ever about what generates and maintains safe emotional bonds over the long term. In an interesting study of couples married 10 years or longer led by Dr. Daniel O'Leary of Stony Brook University, respondents were asked how in love with their partner they were on a scale of 1 to 7 where 1 was "not at all in love," and 7 was "very intensely in love." Surprisingly, 46.3 percent of women and 49 percent of men reported being "very intensely in love." It's not uncommon for partners in long-term relationships to report the same intensities of being in love as those who are newly in love. In other words, it's worth working for.

KNOWING HOW TO MOVE FORWARD

One of my favorite quotes, of uncertain origin, is, "We cannot go back and start over, but we can begin now, and make a new ending." Nowhere is this more applicable than in long-term romantic relationships.

One of the most important things couples can do to move forward in improved relationships is to articulate a narrative for how their relationship has improved over time. Throughout therapy, I will routinely ask couples to describe "what has been better" and where they are "getting the most stuck." We address the current levels of distress by facilitating positive emotional bonding experiences until those experiences move to the forefront of the couple's story, replacing old narratives. The couple over time gains a sense of efficacy for how they are staying out of their negative patterns, and for how they can repair lapses in the relationship.

> *We cannot go back and start over, but we can begin now, and make a new ending.*

LAMAR AND LOUISE OVERCOME THEIR NEGATIVE CYCLES

Lamar and Louise were a couple in their mid-seventies who had been married for over 50 years. When they first came in, I had little hope that I would be able to change their enduring, long-term negative patterns. This isn't because I had an ageist bias, but because both spoke of each other in such negative, hopeless terms when we first met. There seemed to be little goodwill in the relationship. It seemed to me that they didn't like each other enough to even try to be different, and I proceeded with only marginal hope that I could help them feel happier in their marriage.

Not only did this couple change their patterns, much to my delight, but they did so in less than twelve sessions. They were curious learners and worked very hard at understanding the emotions driving their negative patterns. Lamar was determined to increase his emotional presence and began staying engaged with his wife when previously he took a withdrawing and avoidant stance. Instead of disappearing at the first sign of her emotions, he became curious about her pain. Then, he started describing some of his own hurt and fearful emotions to Louise.

She had always thought he wasn't even capable of having empathy and was sure it was because of his "emotionally stunted" childhood. However, his level of engagement reduced her anxiety, so she could reach out to him from a softer place than before. She could talk about her insecurities in a way that helped him understand that her distress was a result of caring about him so much, not that he was just a disappointment. Their description of change was consistent with the goals in couples therapy and they described having a completely different marriage. They both expressed sadness about not having figured out their negative patterns sooner, but appreciated that they could still model a healthier relationship for their grandchildren.

Finding Your Narrative

Write a joint narrative for how the relationship was before and how it is different now:

1. We were getting stuck before when: ....

....

....

....

2. We have learned how to: ....

....

....

....

3. We can remind ourselves that it is us against the negative patterns by:

....

....

....

4. We can be more empathic with each other by remembering that: ....

....

....

....

5. One thing we want to continue working on is: ....

....

....

....

Know Your Danger Signs

Even though couples may have resolved enduring negative patterns, they are likely to continue to have vulnerabilities that can trigger emotional reactivity. Remind yourselves of situations in which proceeding with caution and slowing down are important. On each of these signs, write down your and your partner's vulnerabilities to watch for specifically:

Imagining a Future Together

One strategy commonly used by therapists is to advise couples to imagine a future together. This sends an implicit message that they are working together on building a long-term relationship. Answer these questions:

1. Over the next _____ (weeks/month/year), one thing I really want to

    do with you is: _____

    _____

    _____

    _____

2. _____ (months/years) from now, I am hoping that we: _____

    _____

    _____

    _____

3. _____ (months/years) from now, I am hoping that we: _____

    _____

    _____

    _____

4. _____ (years) from now, I am hoping that we: _____

    _____

    _____

    _____

IMPORTANCE OF RITUALS

One way to prevent future disconnection is to create predictable rituals. Rituals have long been a tool in marriage and family therapy to bring meaning to relationships. They are coordinated, repeated routines with special significance and are designed to cement connection. They foster safety because they are predictable, they provide a framework for a joint identity, they increase positive memories, and they tend to reduce anxiety overall in couple and family systems. They don't need to be elaborate, but couples reap the most benefits when they are routine.

An example of basic rituals between couples are rituals for greetings and goodbyes. As a personal example, I have vivid memories from growing up of the garage door going up each evening, signaling my father's arrival home from work. My parents modeled a loving relationship of mutual support, and one of the most profound memories I have is of my father walking in the door, shouting a warm and enthusiastic, "Is everybody happy?" and finding my mother to kiss on the cheek. Even in her most stressful moments home with six children, his predictable ritual elicited a smile from her on most nights. I remember I felt a sense of safety I had from his expressing affection not to just us children, but to my mother. Since my parents have passed away, my husband sometimes makes me laugh by walking in the door and trying to imitate my father's greeting, so the ritual continues to be the gift that keeps on giving.

> *A ritual works best when there are simple guidelines for how the ritual time should be used and a specific end point is defined.*

Other types of rituals are setting up specific space for having time to check-in or talk together alone. I remember a couple that had a ritual for walking around the block together when one of them arrived home, so they could de-stress and touch base. Another couple routinely enjoyed a smoothie together in the morning before work while they took time to check in with each other. Dr. Doherty suggests building the ritual around times associated with regular family traditions like meals, because it will be easier to stick to them than if they're at a random time not linked to a regular practice. A ritual works best when there are simple guidelines for how the ritual time should be used and a specific end point is defined.

When they take the time, couples come up with excellent ideas for creative rituals. The following are rituals couples have reported to me:

1. One couple that takes mini-vacations alone always plans their next trip together on the way home so they have something to look forward to.

2. One man always brings his partner his favorite candy bar on the same day every month.

3. One couple plans a 30-minute meeting once a week to check in on the state of their relationship, sharing what is going well and what they would like to keep improving.

4. One couple takes a monthly religious trip to their local place of worship to remind themselves of their relationship goals.

5. One couple looks for an unofficial quirky national holiday each month, like "National Burrito Day," or "National Picnic Day," and plans a date around it.

Exercise 9.4

Practicing Rituals

1. List rituals you remember from your family growing up that you would like to keep:_____
    _____

2. List one special thing you can do daily to greet each other:_____
    _____

3. One way we could carve out time for our relationship regularly is:_____
    _____

4. List one thing you can do when one of you is leaving the house:_____
    _____

5. List one thing you can do when one of you arrives home after a day of separation:_____
    _____

6. List one thing you can do at bedtime to reinforce the importance of the relationship:_____
    _____

7. What special occasions (anniversaries, birthdays, special holidays, quirky days) would you like to celebrate regularly?_____
    _____

8. Are there any regular connecting rituals you would like to implement for weekends?_____
    _____

9. Can you think of any other rituals that you want to incorporate into your couple relationship? If so, what?_____
    _____

Novel Dating

One simple way couples can maintain relationship satisfaction is by finding new adventures to go on together. Researchers found that couples who intentionally tried new things together had a significant increase in relationship satisfaction compared to couples who engaged in dating-as-usual.

1. Recall a memory of something you tried with your partner that created a sense of excitement:

    ....

    ....

    ....

2. What is one thing you have been wanting to try?

    ....

    ....

    ....

3. What is one thing your partner has been wanting to try?

    ....

    ....

    ....

4. How can you establish a routine of trying new things in your relationship?

    ....

    ....

    ....

Savoring Positive Experiences

Recent research related to savoring positive experiences, which means focusing on and drawing attention to positive emotions, can be particularly helpful during stressful times. It's a form of positive coping. Even if couples don't have stress within the relationship, they are bound to be impacted by external stressors, such as economic difficulty, illness, death, extended family conflict, parenting issues, moving, etc. Anticipating a strategy for dealing with these times can be helpful. Negative emotions can be absorbing, so this upregulation of positive emotions is suggested to moderate negativity.

Savoring strategies:

1. Take turns choosing three photos from your history that demonstrate moments of happiness.

2. Write down three qualities you particularly admire about your partner. Share these qualities and give examples.

3. Write down three things you are grateful for that have come from your relationship as a couple. Answers can include individual skills developed while learning to work with a partner.

4. Plan an event for the near future. Write down the positive emotions you have when thinking about this event.

5. Write down three bucket-list items you would like to accomplish.

6. Recall a favorite memory from the past. Reminisce about this positive event in detail, sharing fond memories.

BIANCA AND RAUL AFTER EFT

I recently received a text from a woman I had seen in therapy with her husband several years ago. At the time, Bianca came in with her husband, Raul, because she found out that he had been hiding a pornography habit for several years, and she felt understandably betrayed because she had gone to great lengths to work on their sexual connection. She was deeply wounded and struggled with the belief that she would "never be enough," and could not "compete with pornography." Raul made significant shifts to be open and transparent, and had not viewed pornography for a few years, but Bianca still struggled with reaching out to him for closeness or comfort because she reported that she had "put up a wall" and wasn't able to take it down.

We worked on the process outlined in this workbook, beginning with delineating their cycle, which had been in play for over a decade. They learned new ways of understanding core emotions and slowly taking risks to articulate their fears and reach out for emotional connection. Instead of suppressing emotions, Raul began telling Bianca he felt vulnerable as a potential disappointment and failure to her, and he worried she would leave him. In turn, Bianca told him that she was worried that he really wanted someone besides her and needed reassurance about her value to him.

Over a few months, they made observable changes in their interactions in therapy. They both began turning to each other for reassurance and comfort, and tried very hard to be accessible, responsive, and engaged with each other and united against the forces that threatened their relationship. She reported feeling much safer through having these experiences with him, and he reported feeling more hopeful, since she wasn't as closed off from him.

A few years later, Bianca sent me a text explaining that she and Raul were still using the tools they learned in therapy and were excited to model better patterns for their children. She said their oldest child was getting married, and they were confident about providing him with an understanding of how to defeat negative cycles that could have helped them earlier in their marriage. I was beyond thrilled to hear about this success and its impact on future generations. Bianca and Raul were an excellent example of a couple prioritizing their relationship and staying unified. When I asked Bianca what she thought had helped them stay connected for the two years since I had seen them, she shared examples of rituals and practices that I've included in this chapter. They still employed rituals for leaving and coming home, regular date nights, and planning into the future. Whenever I hear one of these stories of enduring change, it makes my whole job worth it.

TYING IT TOGETHER

Just like it takes healthy habits to maintain physical health, it requires effort to keep a relationship strong. We live in a busy, distracting world. It seems nearly impossible to keep a relationship strong without purposefulness. Relationships are always challenging, and there is no magical formula for relationship bliss. However, just like anything else, applying energy to promote healthy connection has benefits for individuals, families, and communities at large.

Key points:

- To maintain gains, it's important for couples to be intentional.

- It helps for couples to articulate a narrative for what the relationship was like before and what it will be like going forward now that they have learned about ways to stay connected.

- It helps couples to plan joint goals for the future.

- It helps couples to review their potential vulnerabilities to protect themselves against future disconnection.

- Couples can increase happiness by doing new things together.

- Couples can upregulate positive emotions by actively remembering happy times and choosing new adventures for themselves.

A Final Word

I am frequently asked if my job isn't depressing because I am dealing with so much couple conflict all the time. I can honestly say that I love what I do, and that I can usually inspire hope in my couples when both partners are committed to improving the relationship.

Change is a process, and it sometimes happens in almost indiscernible increments. Every couple is different, and predicting specific couple change is impossible, but identifying potential change and seeing it unfold so that couples restructure their relationships is consistent and exciting. Wherever couples are in the process of therapy, I can see my way through to healthier patterns and increased emotional safety for them if they keep working on the principles outlined in EFT.

As a couples therapist as well as a supervisor for many therapists working with couples, I believe that every couple I have watched enact positive change has done so by learning to use the tools presented in this workbook and in the greater EFT community. This community provides a solid foundation for therapists and couples for education about the universal principles of attachment, emotion, and experience. My biggest discouragements in therapy are linked to couples believing they are too distressed to fix the patterns, often because they are in so much pain. However, I believe there is always hope where there is desire and willingness to change.

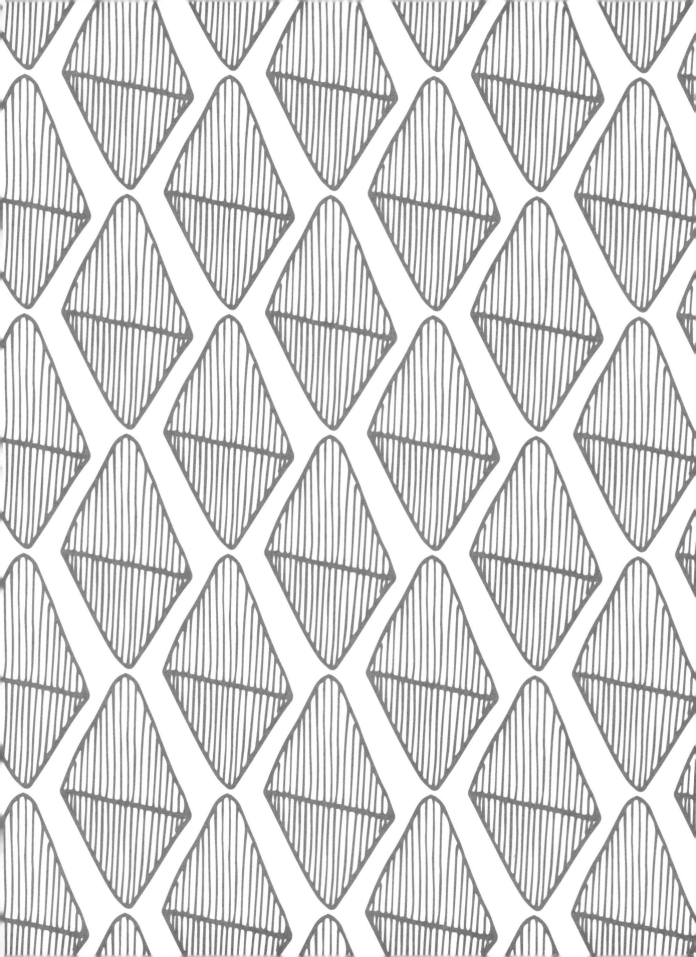

Glossary

accessibility, responsiveness, and engagement (A.R.E.): An acronym created by Sue Johnson describing behaviors present in a secure partner relationship

anxious attachment: An attachment style in which individuals tend to be fearful about being loved and maintain a hypervigilant style of seeking closeness and reassurance, which can sometimes feel aggressive or demanding to a partner

attachment figures: The proximal people who offer reliable support and become a secure base from which to explore the world and take risks to build competency; these people offer a refuge or safe haven, providing comfort in times of stress

attachment injury: A severe violation of trust that brings the entire nature of the relationship into question and diminishes safety, the lack of safety coming from the sense that one doesn't know one's partner as well as previously thought

attachment style: A set of predictable, repeated behaviors that individuals employ to manage distress when their bonded relationships are threatened

attachment theory: An explanation of human behavior based on the assumption that human beings are born helpless and are primally driven to seek safe, predictable responses to their physical and emotional needs in order to establish a positive sense of self and efficacy, and to learn the flexibility and responsiveness necessary to maintain close relationships

avoidant attachment: An attachment style in which individuals tend to suppress or deactivate their own emotional needs from others and instead rely on themselves, giving them the tendency to avoid closeness in close personal relationships

circular causality: A feedback loop in which a series of causes and effects reciprocally leads back to the original cause, thus generating ongoing patterns with no clear linear cause and effect; a relational view of events

core emotions: Emotions that underlie and drive the more obvious coping emotions; for example, anger is often a coping emotion fueled by a core emotion of hurt or fear

co-regulation: The ability to reach out to one's partner when distressed for support and to receive reassurance that one is not alone, facilitating a sense of calm and safety

dependency paradox: The reality that the more one feels secure about receiving predictable, reliable responses from an attachment figure when they express emotional need, the more they will be able to function autonomously

disorganized attachment: A style of attachment in which individuals alternate between anxious and avoidant attachment styles

emotional intelligence: The ability to have awareness about, label, regulate, and understand emotions in oneself and in others, thus increasing empathy

internal working model: A mentally represented template that forms expectations about close interpersonal relationships, thus shaping behavior for how people bring themselves into and respond in relationships

negative cycle: A predictable pattern of couple behaviors that develop over time as couples anticipate attachment responses and employ coping mechanisms to deal with distress; with the whole being greater than the sum of its parts, the pattern of interaction in essence seems to take over the relationship

pair-bonded relationships: A relatively permanent social union between two partners, often monogamous with an exclusive sexual component

protest-protest cycles: A couple relational pattern in which one partner protests, blames, or attacks the other partner to deal with distress, and the other partner matches the behavior by countering with equivalent or higher protest, blame, or attacking, thus keeping the couple stuck in their highly reactive emotions

pursue-withdraw cycle: The most common couple relational pattern in which one partner protests relational disconnection with an escalation of behaviors seeking reassurance, while the other partner responds to the hyper activation of the attachment system and perceived conflict by turning away, withdrawing, and avoiding interaction; thus, the styles tend to polarize the couple and the cycle becomes paradoxically self-maintaining

raw spots: Special emotional sensitivities due to a previous emotional event that is likely related to the current emotional event, putting an individual on guard and increasing their reactivity in a given situation

reactive emotions: Emotions employed to cope with deeper emotions, often to protect oneself; for example, anger is frequently a reactive emotion used to cope with more vulnerable emotions like hurt and fear

sealed-off sex: A type of sex conceptualized by Dr. Sue Johnson in which the overall focus is on physical sensation and performance without concomitant emotional connection

secure attachment: A style of attachment in which individuals have positive views and expectations of self and relationships, leading to increased emotional regulation and behavioral flexibility in managing inevitable ruptures with others

secure bonds: Mutually reciprocal patterns between couples in which they can reach out for emotional support and expect predictable, supportive responses, thus engendering a relationship of effective dependence, in which the confidence about receiving a response from each other also facilitates autonomous behaviors and comfortable independence

solace sex: A type of sex conceptualized by Dr. Sue Johnson in which a partner seeks sexual connection to soothe anxious doubts and fears about the relationship

synchrony sex: A type of sex conceptualized by Dr. Sue Johnson in which partners perpetuate a mutual exchange

of both physical and emotional closeness and responsiveness, increasing an environment of safety and exploration

withdraw-withdraw cycle: A pattern of behaviors in which both individuals have turned away from each other for attachment responses, thus creating distance in the relationship, sometimes developing when a pursuing partner becomes fatigued from seeking connection and ends up turning away, meaning the withdraw-withdraw cycle can sometimes be a former pursue-withdraw cycle

Resources

Recommended Reading

Emotionally Focused Couple Therapy for Dummies by Brent Bradley and James Furrow (2013), Mississauga, ON: John Wiley & Sons.

An Emotionally Focused Workbook for Couples: The Two of Us by Veronica Kallos-Lilly and Jennifer Fitzgerald (2015), New York: Routledge.

Hold Me Tight: Seven Conversations for a Lifetime of Love by Dr. Sue Johnson (2008), New York: Little, Brown Spark.

Love Sense: The Revolutionary New Science of Romantic Relationships by Dr. Sue Johnson (2013), New York: Little, Brown and Company.

Websites

drsuejohnson.com—Here you can read Dr. Sue Johnson's blog entries, watch videos, and access other resources related to EFT.

holdmetightonline.com—This is a site where you can access Dr. Sue Johnson's workshop program for couples.

iceeft.com—The International Centre for Excellence in Emotionally Focused Therapy. They have lots of resources for finding a trained therapist in your area, finding online therapy programs, and reading about current EFT research.

References

Chapter One

Ainsworth, Mary D. Salter. *Patterns of Attachment: A Psychological Study of the Strange Situation.* London: Psychology Press, 1978/2015.

Bowlby, John. *Attachment and Loss*, volume 1: Attachment. New York: Basic Books. 1969/1982.

Finkel, Eli J. *The All-or-Nothing Marriage: How the Best Marriages Work.* New York: Dutton, 2017.

Fraley, R. Chris. "Attachment in Adulthood: Recent Developments, Emerging Debates, and Future Directions." 2019. *Annual Review of Psychology* 70: 401–422. doi.org/10.1146/annurev-psych-010418-102813.

Hazan, Cindy, and Phillip Shaver. "Romantic Love Conceptualized as an Attachment Process." 1987. *Journal of Personality and Social Psychology* 52, no. 3: 511–524. doi.org/10.1037/0022-3514.52.3.511 (subscription required).

Johnson, Sue. *Hold Me Tight: Seven Conversations for a Lifetime of Love.* New York: Little, Brown Spark, 2008.

Johnson, Sue. *Love Sense: The Revolutionary New Science of Romantic Relationships.* New York: Little, Brown and Company, 2013.

Johnson, Susan M., and Valerie E. Whiffen, ed. *Attachment Processes in Couple and Family Therapy.* New York: The Guilford Press, 2003.

Lewis, C. S. *The Four Loves.* San Francisco: HarperOne, 1960, 2017.

Moser, Melissa Burgess, Susan M. Johnson, Tracy L. Dalgleish, Marie-France Lafontaine, Stephanie A. Wiebe, and Giorgio A. Tasca. "Changes in Relationship-Specific Attachment in Emotionally Focused Couples Therapy." 2015. *Journal of Marital and Family Therapy* 42 (2): 231–245. doi.org/10.1111/jmft.12139 (subscription required).

Sandberg, Jonathan G., Dean M. Busby, Susan M. Johnson, and Keitaro Yoshida. "The Brief Accessibility, Responsiveness, and Engagement (BARE) Scale: A Tool for Measuring Attachment Behavior in Couple Relationships." 2012. *Family Process* 51 (4): 512–526. doi.org/10.1111/j.1545-5300.2012.01422.x (subscription required).

Wallin, David J. *Attachment in Psychotherapy.* New York: The Guilford Press, 2017.

Chapter Two

Brubacher, Lorrie L. *Stepping into Emotionally Focused Couple Therapy: Key Ingredients of Change.* London: Karnac Books, Ltd, 2018.

Gottman, John M. *The Science of Trust: Emotional Attunement for Couples.* New York: W. W. Norton & Company, 2011.

Johnson, Sue. *Hold Me Tight: Seven Conversations for a Lifetime of Love.* New York: Little, Brown Spark, 2008.

Johnson, Susan M. *Attachment Theory in Practice.* New York: The Guilford Press, 2019.

Johnson, Susan M. *The Practice of Emotionally Focused Therapy: Creating Connection.* New York: Routledge, 2019.

Johnson, Susan M., Lorrie Brubacher, James L. Furrow, Alison Lee, Gail Palmer, Kathryn Rheem, and Scott Woolley. *Becoming an Emotionally Focused Couples Therapist: The Workbook.* New York: Routledge, 2017.

Chapter Three

Barrett, Lisa Feldman. *How Emotions are Made: The Secret Life of the Brain.* Boston: Houghton Mifflin Harcourt, 2017.

Cozolino, Louis. *The Neuroscience of Human Relationships: Attachment and the Developing Social Brain.* New York: W. W. Norton & Company, 2014.

Darwin, Charles. *The Expression of the Emotions in Man and Animals.* London: Penguin Publishing, 1872/2009.

Davila, Joanne, Haley Wodarczyk, and Vickie Bhatia. "Positive Emotional Expression Among Couples: The Role of Romantic Competence." 2017. *Couple and Family Psychology: Research and Practice* 6, no. 2: 94–105. doi.org/10.1037/cfp0000077 (subscription required).

Ekman, Paul. 2003. *Emotions Revealed.* New York: Times Books, 2003.

Fishbane, Mona DeKoven. *Loving with the Brain in Mind: Neurobiology & Couple Therapy.* New York: W. W. Norton & Company, 2003.

Fosha, Diana. *The Transforming Power of Affect: A Model for Accelerated Change.* New York: Basic Books, 2000.

Johnson, Susan M., Melissa Burgess Moser, Lane Beckes, Andra Smith, Tracy Dalgleish, Rebecca Halchuk, Karen Hasselmo, Paul S. Greenman, Zul Merali, and James A. Coan. "Soothing the Threatened Brain: Leveraging Contact Comfort with Emotionally Focused Couples Therapy." 2014. *PLoS ONE* 9(8), e105489. https://doi.org/10.1371/journal.pone.0079314.

Mikulincer, Mario, Phillip R. Shaver, and Dana Pereg. "Attachment Theory and Affect Regulation: The Dynamics, Development, and Cognitive Consequences of Attachment-Related Strategies." 2003. *Motivation and Emotion,* 27, no. 2: 77–102. doi.org/10.1023/A:1024515519160 (subscription required).

Panksepp, Jaak. "Brain Emotional Systems and Qualities of Mental Life: From Animal Models of Affect to Implications for Psychotherapeutics." In *The Healing*

Power of Emotion, edited by Diana Fosha, Daniel J. Siegel, and Marion Solomon, 1–26. New York: W. W. Norton & Company, 2009.

Porges, Stephen W., and Deb A. Dana. *Clinical Applications of the Polyvagal Theory: The Emergence of Polyvagal-Informed Therapies.* New York: W. W. Norton & Co., 2018.

Siegel, Daniel J. *The Mindful Therapist.* New York: W. W. Norton & Co., 2010.

Tugade, Michele M., Barbara L. Frederickson, and Lisa Feldman Barrett. "Psychological Resilience and Positive Emotional Granularity: Examining the Benefits of Positive Emotions on Coping and Health." 2004. *Journal of Personality* 72 (6): 1161–1190. doi.org/10.1111/j.1467-6494.2004.00294.x (subscription required).

Chapter Four

Bradley, Brent, and James Furrow. "Inside Blamer Softening: Maps and Missteps." 2007. *Journal of Systemic Therapies* 26, no. 4: 25–43. guilfordjournals.com/doi/pdfplus/10.1521/jsyt.2007.26.4.25

Bradley, Brent, and James Furrow. "Toward a Mini-Theory of the Blamer Softening Event: Tracking the Moment-by-Moment Process." 2004. *Journal of Marital and Family Therapy* 30 (2): 233–246. doi.org/10.1111/j.1752-0606.2004.tb01236.x (subscription required).

Fosha, Diana. *The Transforming Power of Affect: A Model for Accelerated Change.* New York: Basic Books, 2000.

Johnson, Sue. *Hold Me Tight: Seven Conversations for a Lifetime of Love.* New York: Little, Brown Spark, 2008.

Johnson, Susan M. *The Practice of Emotionally Focused Therapy: Creating Connection.* New York: Routledge, 2019.

Moser, Melissa Burgess, Susan M. Johnson, Tracy L. Dalgleish, Stephanie A. Wiebe, and Giorgio A. Tasca. "The Impact of Blamer-Softening on Romantic Attachment in Emotionally Focused Couples Therapy." 2018. *Journal of Marital and Family Therapy* 44 (4): 640–654. doi.org/10.1111/jmft.12284 (subscription required).

Porges, Stephen W., and Deb A. Dana. *Clinical Applications of the Polyvagal Theory: The Emergence of Polyvagal-Informed Therapies.* New York: W. W. Norton & Co., 2018.

Chapter Five

Greenberg, Leslie S. "Emotion-Focused Therapy: A Clinical Synthesis." 2010. *Focus: The Journal of Lifelong Learning in Psychiatry* 8 (1): 32–42. doi.org/10.1176/foc.8.1.foc32 (subscription required).

Johnson, Sue. *Hold Me Tight: Seven Conversations for a Lifetime of Love*. New York: Little, Brown Spark, 2008.

Johnson, Sue. *The Hold Me Tight Program: Conversations for Connection; Facilitator's Guide for Small Groups*. Canada: International Center for Excellence in Emotionally Focused Therapy, 2009.

Johnson, Susan M. *The Practice of Emotionally Focused Therapy: Creating Connection*. New York: Routledge, 2019.

Johnson, Susan M., Lorrie Brubacher, James L. Furrow, Alison Lee, Gail Palmer, Kathryn Rheem, and Scott Woolley. *Becoming an Emotionally Focused Couples Therapist: The Workbook*. New York: Routledge, 2017.

Porges, Stephen W., and Deb A. Dana. *Clinical Applications of the Polyvagal Theory: The Emergence of Polyvagal-Informed Therapies*. New York: W. W. Norton & Co., 2018.

Chapter Six

Dalgleish, Tracy L., Susan M. Johnson, Melissa Burgess Moser, Stephanie A. Wiebe, and Giorgio A. Tasca. "Predicting Key Change Events in Emotionally Focused Couple Therapy." 2015. *Journal of Marital and Family Therapy* 41, no. 3: 260–275. doi.org/10.1111/jmft.12101 (subscription required).

Fosha, Diana. *The Transforming Power of Affect: A Model for Accelerated Change*. New York: Basic Books, 2000.

Johnson, Sue. *Hold Me Tight: Seven Conversations for a Lifetime of Love*. New York: Little, Brown Spark, 2008.

Johnson, Sue. *The Hold Me Tight Program: Conversations for Connection; Facilitator's Guide for Small Groups*. Canada: International Center for Excellence in Emotionally Focused Therapy, 2009.

Johnson, Susan M., Lorrie Brubacher, James L. Furrow, Alison Lee, Gail Palmer, Kathryn Rheem, and Scott Woolley. *Becoming an Emotionally Focused Couples Therapist: The Workbook*. New York: Routledge, 2017.

Schade, Lori Cluff. "A Longitudinal View of the Association Between Therapist Behaviors and Couples' In-Session Process: An Observational Pilot Study of Emotionally Focused Couples Therapy." PhD Dissertation, Brigham Young University, 2013.

Chapter Seven

Brubacher, Lorrie L. *Stepping into Emotionally Focused Couple Therapy: Key Ingredients of Change*. London: Karnac Books, Ltd., 2018.

Fincham, Frank D., R. H. Steven Beach, and Joanne Davila. "Forgiveness and Conflict Resolution in Marriage." 2004. *Journal of Family Psychology* 18, no. 1: 72–81. doi.org/10.1037/0893-3200.18.1.72 (subscription required).

Gottman, John M., and Nan Silver. *The Seven Principles for Making Marriage Work: A Practical Guide from the Country's Foremost Relationship Expert.* New York: Crown, 1999.

Halchuk, Rebecca E., Judy A. Makinen, and Susan M. Johnson. "Resolving Attachment Injuries in Couples Using Emotionally Focused Therapy: A Three-Year Follow-Up." 2010. *Journal of Couple & Relationship Therapy* 9 (1): 31–47. doi.org/10.1080/15332690903473069.

Johnson, Susan M. 2005. *Emotionally Focused Couple Therapy with Trauma Survivors: Strengthening Attachment Bonds.* New York: The Guilford Press, 2005.

Johnson, Sue. *Hold Me Tight: Seven Conversations for a Lifetime of Love.* New York: Little, Brown Spark, 2008.

Makinen, Judy A., and Lorie Ediger. "Rebuilding Bonds After the Traumatic Impact of Infidelity." In *The Emotionally Focused Casebook: New Directions in Treating Couples,* edited by James L. Furrow, Susan M. Johnson, and Brent A. Bradley, 247–268. New York: Routledge, 2011.

Meneses, Catalina Woldarsky, and Leslie S. Greenberg. "Interpersonal Forgiveness in Emotion-Focused Couples therapy: Relating Process to Outcome." 2014. *American Journal of Family Therapy* 40 (1): 49–67. doi.org/10.1080/15332690903473069 (subscription required).

Schade, Lori Cluff, and Jonathan G. Sandberg. "Healing the Attachment Injury of Marital Infidelity Using Emotionally Focused Couples Therapy: A Case Illustration." 2012. *The American Journal of Family Therapy* 40 (5): 434–444. doi.org/10.1080/01926187.2011.631374 (subscription required).

Zuccarini, Dino, Susan M. Johnson, Tracy L. Dalgleish, and Judy A. Makinen. "Forgiveness and Reconciliation in Emotionally Focused Therapy for Couples: The Client Change Process and Therapist Interventions." 2013. *Journal of Marital and Family Therapy* 39, no. 2: 148–162. doi.org/10.1111/j.1752-0606.2012.00287.x (subscription required).

Chapter Eight

Busby, Dean M., Veronica Hanna-Walker, and Jeremy B. Yorgason. "A Closer Look at Attachment, Sexuality, and Couple Relationships." 2020. *Journal of Social and Personal Relationships,* 37, no. 4: 1362–1385. doi.org/10.1177/0265407519896022 (subscription required).

Girard, Abby, and Scott Woolley. "Using Emotionally Focused Therapy to Treat Sexual Desire Discrepancy in Couples." 2017. *Journal of Sex & Marital Therapy,*

43, no. 8: 720–735. doi.org/10.1080/0092623X.2016.1263703 (subscription required).

Holt-Lunstad, Julianne, W. A. Birmingham, and Kathleen C. Light. "Influence of a 'Warm Touch' Support Enhancement Intervention among Married Couples on Ambulatory Blood Pressure, Oxytocin, Alpha Amylase, and Cortisol." 2008. *Psychosomatic Medicine* 70 (9): 976–985. doi.org/10.1097/PSY.0b013e318187aef7 (subscription required).

Johnson, Sue. *Hold Me Tight: Seven Conversations for a Lifetime of Love*. New York: Little, Brown Spark, 2008.

Johnson, Sue. *Love Sense: The Revolutionary New Science of Romantic Relationships*. New York: Little, Brown and Company, 2013.

Johnson, Susan, and Dino Zuccarini. "Integrating Sex and Attachment in Emotionally Focused Couples Therapy." 2010. *Journal of Marital and Family Therapy* 36, no. 4: 431–445. doi.org/10.1111/j.1752-0606.2009.00155.x (subscription required).

Kleinplatz, Peggy J., and A. Dana Ménard. *Magnificent Sex: Lessons from Extraordinary Lovers*. New York: Routledge, 2020.

Love, Heather, Rachel M. Moore, and Natalie A. Stanish. "Emotionally Focused Therapy for Couples Recovering from Sex Addiction." 2016. *Sexual and Relationship Therapy* 31, no. 2: 176–189. doi.org/10.1080/14681994.2016.1142522 (subscription required).

McCarthy, Barry. *Sex Made Simple: Clinical Strategies for Sexual Issues in Therapy*. Wisconsin: PESI, 2015.

McCarthy, Barry, and Emily McCarthy. *Enhancing Couple Sexuality: Creating an Intimate and Erotic Bond*. New York: Routledge, 2019.

Mikulincer, Mario, and Phillip R. Shaver. "A Behavioral Systems Perspective on the Psychodynamics of Attachment and Sexuality." In *Attachment and Sexuality*, edited by Diana Diamond, Sidney J. Blatt, and Joseph D. Lichtenberg, 51–78. New York: The Analytic Press, 2007.

Resnick, Stella. *Body-to-Body Intimacy*. New York: Routledge, 2019.

Wiebe, Stephanie A., Cass Elliott, Susan M. Johnson, Melissa Burgess Moser, Tracy L. Dalgleish, Marie-France Lafontaine, and Giorgio A. Tasca. "Attachment Change in Emotionally Focused Therapy and Sexual Satisfaction Outcomes in a Two-year Follow-up Study." 2019. *Journal of Couple & Relationship Therapy,* 18, no. 1: 1–21. doi.org/10.1080/15332691.2018.1481799 (subscription required).

Yoo, Hana, Suzanne Bartle-Haring, Randal D. Day, and Rashmi Gangamma. "Couple Communication, Emotional, and Sexual Intimacy, and Relationship Satisfaction." 2014. *Journal of Sex & Marital Therapy,* 40, no. 4: 275–293. doi.org/10.1080/0092623X.2012.751072 (subscription required).

Zuccarini, Dino, and Leigh Karos. "Emotionally Focused Therapy for Gay and Lesbian Couples: Strong Identities, Strong Bonds." In *The Emotionally Focused Casebook: New Directions in Treating Couples,* edited by James L. Furrow, Susan M. Johnson, and Brent A. Bradley, 317–342. New York: Routledge, 2011.

Chapter Nine

Aron, Arthur, Christina C. Norman, Elaine N. Aron, Colin McKenna, and Richard E. Heyman. "Couples' Shared Participation in Novel and Arousing Activities and Experienced Relationship Quality." 2000. *Journal of Personality and Social Psychology* 78, no. 2: 273–284. doi.org/10.1037//0022-3514.78.2.273 (subscription required).

Coulter, Kimberley, and John M. Malouff. "Effects of an Intervention Designed to Enhance Romantic Relationship Excitement: A Randomized-Control Trial." 2013. *Couple and Family Psychology: Research and Practice* 2, no. 1: 34–44. doi.org/10.1037/a0031719 (subscription required).

Doherty, William J. *Take Back Your Marriage: Sticking Together in a World that Pulls Us Apart.* New York: The Guilford Press, 2013.

Gottman, John M., and Julie Schwartz Gottman. *10 Principles for Doing Effective Couples Therapy.* New York: W. W. Norton & Company, 2015.

Johnson, Sue. *Hold Me Tight: Seven Conversations for a Lifetime of Love.* New York: Little, Brown Spark.2008.

Markman, Howard J., Scott M. Stanley, and Susan L. Blumberg. *Fighting for Your Marriage: A Deluxe Revised Edition of the Classic Best-seller for Enhancing Marriage and Preventing Divorce.* San Francisco: Jossey-Bass, 2010.

O'Leary, K. Daniel, Bianca P. Acevedo, Arthur Aron, Leonie Huddy, and Debra Mashek. "Is Long-Term Love More than a Rare Phenomenon? If So, What Are Its Correlates?" 2012. *Social Psychological and Personality Science* 32 (2): 241–249. doi.org/10.1177/1948550611417015 (subscription required).

Samios, Christina, and Vidushi Khatri. "When Times Get Tough: Savoring and Relationship Satisfaction in Couples Coping with a Stressful Life Event." 2019. *Anxiety, Stress & Coping* 32 (2): 125–140. doi.org/10.1080/10615806.2019 .1570804 (subscription required).

Verstaen, Alice, Claudia M. Haase, Sandy J. Lwi, and Robert W. Levenson. "Age-Related Changes in Emotional Behavior: Evidence from a 13-Year Longitudinal Study of Long-Term Married Couples." 2018. *Emotion* 20 (2): 149–163. doi .org/10.1037/emo0000551 (subscription required).

Index

A

Ainsworth, Mary, 3
All-or-Nothing Marriage, The (Finkel), 1
Anger, 60
Anxious attachment, 9, 14–15, 23, 118
A.R.E. acronym, 20–21, 23, 85
Attachment
    fears, 92–93, 96
    figures, 3–4, 10, 12–13, 92
    injuries, 99–113, 130
    longings, xii, 83, 84, 87, 92
    styles, xii, 8–9, 14–19, 23
    theory, x, xiii, 3, 23
Avoidant attachment, 8, 14, 16–17, 23, 118

B

Bonding conversations, 83–88, 96
Bonds, 4, 7, 23, 43, 117–118, 132, 135
Bowlby, John, 3, 8, 20, 92
Busby, Dean, 20

C

Coan, James, 47
Connection, 3, 8, 27, 46, 65–66, 70, 83, 95–96
Co-regulation, 45–47, 52, 57, 63

D

Darwin, Charles, 43
Dating, 144
De-escalation, xiii, 75–81
Dependency paradox, 11, 94
Disorganized attachment, 14
Doherty, William, 135, 141

E

Ekman, Paul, 43
Emotional intelligence, 45
Emotionally focused couples
    therapy (EFT), viii–xii
Emotional support, xii, 5–6, 10, 12–13, 25, 45
Emotions
    acceptable, 50–51
    and action tendencies, 49, 52, 70
    and attachment fears, 92–93
    bonding conversations
        about, 83–88, 96
    core, 43, 52, 55–63, 105, 146
    positive, x, xiii, 8, 46, 48–49, 51, 83, 85, 136, 145, 147
    raw spots, 65–70, 81
    reactive, 55–63, 76, 88
    regulating, xii, 8, 14, 40, 45–47, 49, 52, 57, 63, 65–66, 75, 77, 85
    responding to, 20, 45, 94, 111
    savoring positive experiences, 145

F

Fears, 18–19, 58, 63, 86–87, 90, 92–93, 95–96, 120, 125, 131, 146
Fincham, Frank, 100
Finkel, Eli, 1
Forgiveness, 99–101, 105–107, 113

G

Gottman, John, 100

H

Happiness, 43, 46, 99, 113, 117, 145, 147
Hazan, Cindy, 3
Healing, 111–113
Hold Me Tight (Johnson), 20, 26, 70, 75, 87, 92
Holt-Lundstad, Julianne, 125

I

Infidelity, ix, xi, 102, 113. *See also*
    Attachment: injuries
Internal working models, 8
Intimacy. *See* Sex and intimacy

J

Johnson, Susan, ix, xii, 4, 20, 26, 29, 31–33, 47, 65, 70, 75, 83, 87, 92, 118

K

Kleinplatz, Peggy, 119, 125

L

Lewis, C. S., 4
LGBTQIA couples, xi

M

Magnificent Sex (Kleinplatz), 119
McCarthy, Barry, 118

N

Narratives, 136, 138, 147
Negative cycles, x, xiii, 19, 25–27, 34–40,
    47, 52, 56–57, 63, 75, 81, 117, 137, 146
  de-escalating, xiii, 75–81
  overcoming, 135–140
  protest-protest, 29–31, 34, 38
  pursue-withdraw, 27–29, 34, 40, 121
  role of core vs. reactive emotions, 55–58
  and sex, 121–124
  withdraw-withdraw, 31–33, 34, 40

O

O'Leary, Daniel, 135

P

Pain, 112–113
Protest-protest cycles, 29–31, 34, 38
Pursue-withdraw cycles, 27–29, 34, 40, 121

R

Raw spots, 65–74, 81
Reassurance, 4, 11, 18, 57, 61, 89–96, 105–106,
    111–112, 118, 121, 123–124, 131, 146
Rituals, 141–143, 146

S

Sandberg, Jonathan, 20
Savoring strategies, 145
Sealed-off sex, 118, 120
Secure attachment, xii–xiii,
    8–9, 14, 18, 23, 94, 118
Sensitivities, xiii, 65–74, 81
Sex and intimacy, 117–118, 132
  attachment injuries, 99, 130, 146
  increasing comfort during, 126–127
  negative cycles and, 121–124
  peak experiences, 119, 132
  reassurance and safety, 131–132, 141
  sexual styles, 118–120
  warm touch, 125, 128–129, 132
Shaver, Philip, 3
Solace sex, 118, 120
Synchrony sex, 118–120

T

Take Back Your Marriage (Doherty), 135

V

Vulnerability, 11, 55, 73–74, 84–88,
    120, 125, 130, 132, 139, 146–147

W

Withdraw-withdraw cycles, 31–33
Woolley, Scott, 26

Y

Yoshida, Keitaro, 20

Acknowledgments

I would first like to thank my husband, Steve, my biggest cheerleader, for his constant reassurance and support in the completion of this project, and for going along with my crazy ideas, like skydiving. He really is my hero. I'm also eternally grateful to my children and their spouses, Kevin and Savanna, Ryan and Hilary, Trevor and Anne, Tyler, Nicole, and Scott and Krista for being patient with my inaccessibility whenever I am focused on a writing deadline, and for making me laugh. My grandchildren, Landry (Landry Bug), Georgia (Her Georgeness), Steven (Stee the Wee), Sutton (Sutter Butter), and Frances (Francy Pants), also make me laugh and inspire me with joy every day.

Even though they are gone now, and I miss them every day, I am indebted to both of my parents for modeling secure attachment and teaching me to pursue high educational goals. I often hear my father's warm words as a distant echo, "You're talented, smart, and beautiful. Smile! You can accomplish anything!" I wish he were here so I could apologize for all the times I rolled my eyes at him when he was giving me his motivational speeches. My mother, also brilliant, taught me to love reading, knitting, music, and how to appreciate a good joke. They both taught me to value warmth and humor, which helps in the craziness of running a busy household.

My amazing friend Christy Ogden deserves recognition for reading my rough drafts and giving excellent feedback in addition to listening to me whine when I felt overwhelmed.

I want to acknowledge my most proximal EFT mentors and friends, Scott Woolley and Rebecca Jorgensen, for their diligence in training me and other therapists in the execution of EFT therapy. They have always been kind and encouraging whenever I've had questions and have allowed me to participate in co-therapy to hone my craft.

I'm grateful to Sue Johnson for her scholarship and clinical example in providing the world with better couples therapists. I learned a lot from her in the limited time I received her feedback on my cases at BYU and use her suggestions regularly. I'm also awestruck by the greater EFT community and the mutual support they offer to promote excellent therapy. Brian Sweeting in particular has been an incredibly collaborative partner, offering flexibility, encouragement, and thoughtfulness with his suggestions along the way. His work at the front end of this project in researching EFT was impressively comprehensive, which made my job that much easier.

Lastly, I want to thank my clients, who allow me into some extremely vulnerable spaces.

About the Author

Lori Cluff Schade, PhD, LMFT is a licensed marriage and family therapist, AAMFT-approved supervisor, and EFT-certified supervisor and clinician practicing therapy in Pleasant Grove, Utah. She owns *Compassionate Connections Counseling* and works part-time as adjunct faculty in Brigham Young University's marriage and family therapy department. For over three decades she has been practicing therapy alternately with raising seven children and has published several peer-reviewed articles and a book chapter related to her profession. In her spare time, she runs, cycles, knits, and plays the organ and piano. Her favorite activity is trying anything new. She is grateful for the opportunity to have a career doing what she loves.